Joined by Grace

Program Manual

PREPARING FOR THE SACRAMENTAL JOURNEY OF MARRIAGE

Nihil Obstat and *Imprimatur*: Most Reverend David R. Choby
Bishop of Nashville
May 5, 2016

The *Nihil Obstat* and *Imprimatur* are official declarations that a book or pamphlet is free of doctrinal or moral error. No implication is contained therein that those who have granted the *Nihil Obstat* or *Imprimatur* agree with its contents, opinions, or statements expressed.

Founded in 1865, Ave Maria Press is a ministry of the United States Province of Holy Cross.

www.avemariapress.com

Paperback: ISBN-13 978-1-59471-552-5

Cover and text design by K. H. Bonelli and Katherine J. Ross.

Printed and bound in the United States of America.

Contents

Foreword

At a time when the Church recognizes the importance of marriage preparation as an essential link in the transmission of faith from one generation to the next, John and Teri Bosio give us Joined by Grace: Preparing for the Sacramental Journey of Marriage—an excellent tool to help parishes welcome young couples to marriage and prepare them to embrace their Christian vocation. Joined by Grace incorporates the recommendations surfaced at the two Synods on the Family and addressed by Pope Francis in his apostolic exhortation *Amoris Laetitia* (*The Joy of Love*).

The Holy Father calls us to accompany the engaged to the altar as a community, evangelizing and catechizing them. At the same time, we must strengthen their connection to the life of the parish (*Amoris Laetitia*, 206). Quoting the Synod Fathers, Pope Francis emphasizes the importance of helping the engaged understand the connection between Marriage, Baptism, and the other sacraments of the Church. Joined by Grace assists parish and diocesan leaders in accomplishing all of these goals. It does so while keeping in mind the needs of today's young adults—the millennial generation—many of whom marry non-Catholics and non-believers. The needs of this group are quite distinct from early generations, and many of today's engaged couples require basic catechesis along with a heartfelt and sincere invitation to come to know Jesus Christ and his Church.

What I like most about Joined by Grace is its unique catechetical framework within which Christian married life is presented. Married life is explored through the lens of Christ's loving actions for the Church as experienced in each of the seven sacraments. The sacramental acts of Christ are sources of grace and models of spousal interaction for the couple. In Joined by Grace, engaged couples are reacquainted with or introduced for the first time to the seven sacraments, and from each sacrament, lessons are drawn that address the typical marriage preparation topics such as communication, finances, sexuality, sacramentality, spirituality, and Natural Family Planning. These topics are explored by presenting Church teaching and by exploring practical life skills necessary for building strong marriages. The love of Jesus for the Church in the sacraments becomes the blueprint given to the engaged with which to build their marriages.

This *Program Manual* is specific and full of ideas about how to implement Joined by Grace. This book and the *Mentor Guide, Couple's Book,* program DVD, and the Joined by Grace website together contain all the resources a parish will need to get started with the program, including help for recruiting and training mentor couples and suggestions on how to engage the whole parish community in praying for and supporting the engaged. I recommend Joined by Grace for parishes that want to use marriage preparation as an opportunity for evangelizing, catechizing, and building strong families for tomorrow.

John and Teri Bosio have dedicated many years of their married life to helping couples at various stages of their marriage. Joined by Grace represents the synthesis of their work—their insights about married life and their experiences in marriage ministry. I am proud to introduce this work of theirs to you.

Most Reverend David R. Choby
Bishop of Nashville
July 15, 2016

Introduction

Dear Family Life Ministers,

We have been involved in marriage-and-family ministry for most of our married life, which now spans four decades. It is a ministry we feel called to, and we are glad to have the opportunity to share our own experiences of the ministry and of married life with you, with those who will work alongside you in this crucial work of the Church, and with the engaged couples whom you hope to reach with Joined by Grace. Years ago when we served the Archdiocese of Kansas City in Kansas as family-life coordinators, we were responsible for hosting monthly marriage-preparation retreats and for helping parishes across the archdiocese to recruit and train mentor couples who would open their homes to small groups of engaged couples preparing for marriage. We continue our involvement with marriage preparation as volunteers in the Diocese of Nashville where we now live.

Those getting married today have grown up in a very different culture and have different needs than the engaged couples of fifteen or twenty years ago. And the Church has a far better understanding of what our responsibility is toward them as they prepare for marriage. Perhaps most importantly, they need mentors, companions, people in the parish faithfully living out the vocation of Christian marriage whom they can follow as role models and turn to for guidance. Joined by Grace is built on the vision of marriage preparation as a ministry of encounter and accompaniment, as is described by Pope Francis in his 2016 apostolic exhortation, *Amoris Laetitia* (*The Joy of Love*), 205–216.

Today, most engaged couples seeking marriage in the Church belong to the millennial generation. Millennials are the generation born between 1980 and 2005 by most accountings. According to recent research, millennials are not well versed in their Catholic faith, few attend Mass regularly, and many are not connected in any practical way to a parish community. In addition, a significant number of young Catholics are marrying partners who are not Catholic or not religious, and some of them are cohabiting. Most engaged couples today need not only to be catechized but to be evangelized and connected in positive ways to the life of the Church. They need to be introduced to Jesus Christ and his Church in a most fundamental way. What better way to evangelize than through the powerful personal witness of married couples who struggle and rejoice each day in their vocational calling? What better way to catechize than to explore the sacramental life of the Church and the graces it affords us? What better way to connect the engaged to the life of the Church than inviting them to attend Sunday Mass and asking the members of their parish to pray for them. These three aspects of immediate preparation for marriage lie at the heart of Joined by Grace: Preparing for the Sacramental Journey of Marriage.

> The Synod Fathers agreed on the need to involve the entire community more extensively [in marriage preparation] by stressing the witness of families themselves and by grounding marriage preparation in the process of Christian initiation by bringing out the connection between Marriage, Baptism, and the other sacraments . . . [and] the need for . . . giving couples a genuine experience of participation in ecclesial life.
>
> —Pope Francis, *Amoris Laetitia*, 206

Evangelizing, catechizing and connecting the engaged couples to their faith tradition and community is the three-fold goal of Joined by Grace. Know that you, your engaged couples, and your marriage preparation team are in our prayers.

God bless you,
John and Teri Bosio

1.

Exploring the Vision of Joined by Grace

Genuine spiritual accompaniment always begins and flourishes in the context of service to the mission of evangelization.

—Pope Francis, *Evangelii Gaudium*, 173

Marriage Preparation Is an Opportunity and a Challenge

On the front page of our parish bulletin, along with Mass schedules and times for celebrating the sacrament of Reconciliation and the Baptism of Infants, there is a simple notice: "Marriages: contact Deacon Hans, (phone number), at time of engagement (ASAP)."

"Couples call me," says Deacon Hans, "because someone told them that to get married in the church they need to call me. Their wedding plans are on their mind, and they want to know what they need to do to be married in the parish church."

When a couple contacts the parish to talk about getting married, it is a great opportunity for the Church but it is also a challenge. All that couples seem to want at that moment is to have their wedding in the parish church. But as we who have answered the call to marriage ministry know well, the Church has so much more to offer!

The challenge for all pastoral ministers receiving such calls is to welcome these couples with warm enthusiasm, listen to their stories and their questions, try to understand their fundamental needs, inform them, and guide them without turning them off. The wedding is a huge moment in these couples' lives, and for some reason they want the Church to be a part of it. It is important that the parish staff, especially whoever is the first point of contact—often the parish secretary—be trained in basic hospitality and be well versed in the information couples will want and need to know.

Deacon Hans explains: "Their decision to call the parish is an inkling of faith that is alive." Whoever receives the first call from an engaged couple asking for information about marriage in the Church begins a relationship. This relationship is the beginning of a faith journey.

Joined by Grace is a program designed to help those in ministry meet engaged couples where they are and walk with them to the altar and beyond, while forming them and preparing them to become a sacrament of Christ's love for the Church.

Marriage Preparation: A Ministry of Accompaniment

In our day-to-day conversations we often speak of marriage preparation as a program. However, marriage preparation is first and foremost a ministry. It is a ministry of accompaniment. It is the whole parish community, led by the pastor, walking the engaged couple to the altar, and in the words of Pope Francis, making present to the engaged "the fragrance of Christ's closeness and his personal gaze" (*Evangelii Gaudium,* 169).

Marriage preparation is a ministry of accompaniment that is best described and understood using the gospel story of Jesus and the disciples on the road to Emmaus, found in Luke 24. Joined by Grace helps parishes accompany engaged couples on their journey to marriage following the example of Jesus in the story. Like Jesus we:

1. meet the engaged wherever they are on their journeys, and listen to them,

2. share the Good News of salvation that we know in Jesus Christ,

3. celebrate the Lord's presence with them, especially in the Eucharist, and

4. help them connect or reconnect with the faith tradition and community.

1. We Meet the Engaged Where They Are, and Listen to Them

> Jesus himself drew near and walked with them.
>
> —Luke 24:15

Walking with them and discovering where the engaged are on their journey is the first crucial step to this three-fold ministry of evangelization, catechesis, and incorporation into the life of the Church. You can read more about the millennial generation on pages 7–11 of the *Mentor Guide*, but here are some key highlights.

- Millennials come to marriage later in life than previous generations: age 29 for men and 26.6 for women are average.
- Most of them have attended college and have started a job or career.
- Many are marrying a non-Catholic or someone who is a nonbeliever.
- Many are already living together, and some already have children.
- Many are not going to church regularly.
- Some have attitudes about sex and intimacy that need redirecting. For example, according to a 2007 study, 66.5 percent of young men and 48.7 percent of young women attending high school said that "viewing pornographic materials is an acceptable way to express one's sexuality."[1]

Understanding where these couples are coming from requires that we listen to them with a pastoral ear. This helps us better learn what each couple needs. Pope Francis describes the listening that must take place when we accompany others: "We need to practice the art of listening, which is more than simply hearing. Listening . . . is an openness of heart which makes possible closeness without which genuine spiritual encounter cannot occur" (*Evangelii Gaudium*, 171).

Joined by Grace envisions six key parish ministers called to accompany the engaged, helping them come to know and love Christ by their example, their sharing of the Church's teaching, and their varied levels of interaction. Sometimes these ministries overlap, yet each plays a crucial and distinctive role:

1. the first point of contact (often the parish secretary)
2. the priest or deacon who will witness the couple's marriage vows
3. the Joined by Grace program director or coordinator
4. the mentor couple
5. the wedding planner
6. the whole parish community

More will be said about each of these in chapter 2. Here it is important to note that each person assuming a role in the ministry of marriage preparation must listen, get to know, welcome, and guide the engaged couple in this most fundamental approach to evangelization. As Jesus did for the disciples on the road to Emmaus, we share the Good News beginning with the way we interact with one another.

2. We Share the Good News

In the Gospel of Luke, we read, "He [Jesus] interpreted to them what referred to him in all the scriptures" (Lk 24:27). Just as Jesus catechized the disciples on the road to Emmaus, we take on the ministry of catechizing in marriage preparation. A peek at the demographic profile of millennial Catholics underscores the challenges in approaching this aspect of the ministry.

- Fewer millennials have attended religious education or a Catholic school than previous generations.[2]
- Only 26 percent of millennial Catholics say their views on marriage have been informed by their Catholic faith.[3]

- A lot of catechesis or handing on of the faith happens during Sunday Mass. However, only 10 to 20 percent of millennials attend Mass weekly. This is a significant statistic because, according to the findings of the Center for Applied Research in the Apostolate (CARA), the frequency of Mass attendance correlates positively with a person's views about marriage that are consistent with the views of the Catholic Church.[4] The low Mass attendance by millennials may also explain the next point.
- The majority of millennials believe that a person can be a "good Catholic" without adhering to the Church's teachings on contraception and its teachings about Sunday Mass attendance.[5]

Joined by Grace places great importance on grounding the sacrament of Marriage in the story of our salvation. It does so by tapping into the compelling joy engaged couples experience because of their love for one another. The program frames the couple's love story in the context of the mystery of God's love story—the story of our salvation.

This program communicates to engaged couples the following teachings in the *Couple's Book*, in the small-group or couple-to-couple meetings or weekend retreat, and in the witness videos.

- When God's grace joins two people in the sacrament of Marriage, their love story is merged with God's love story.
- Their love story becomes part of God's love story, and they agree to play a special role in it.
- God the Father becomes their teacher, Jesus becomes their model of love, and the Holy Spirit the source of strength to carry out their role in God's love story.
- Married couples become visible signs in their families and communities of God's love for us. They become living sacraments for the world, conduits of God's saving grace.
- Married couples sustain and nourish their union through participation in the life of the Church, especially celebration of the sacraments of Eucharist and Reconciliation
- They will find in the parish community support and guidance as they grow in their life together as husband and wife.

Once couples understand they are part of a plan that is greater than themselves, their life as married couples takes on a new meaning. It is a sacred vocation, initiated and blessed by God. We read in *Familiaris Consortio*: "Among the elements to be instilled in this journey of faith, which is similar to the catechumenate, there must also be a deeper knowledge of the mystery of Christ and the Church, of the meaning of grace and of the responsibility of Christian marriage" (66).

Joined by Grace grounds its catechesis of the engaged during marriage preparation in the process of Christian initiation by showing the connection between marriage, baptism and the other sacraments, as Pope Francis suggests in *Amoris Laetitia,* 206. Joined by Grace invites engaged couples to focus their attention on the "mystery of Christ and the Church" as we experience it in the seven sacraments. There we find the model of spousal love. In the sacraments, through the actions of the Father, Son, and Holy Spirit, the Church is cleansed, strengthened, nourished, forgiven, healed, and cared for. The sacraments reveal to us the blueprint of God's love, which needs to become the blueprint of love for every couple building a Christian marriage. St. John Paul II pointed to Jesus as the model for married couples when he wrote, "Husbands and wives discover in Christ the point of reference for their spousal love" (*Gratissimam Sane,* 19).

Because we believe that "God's way of loving becomes the measure of human love," as Pope Benedict XVI taught in *Deus Caritas Est,* Joined by Grace is built around what we call "the blueprint of God's love." This plan for love is explored in the six chapters of the *Couple's Book* and in the six meetings with mentors or six segments of a weekend retreat:

1. Welcoming and Accepting: The Grace and Call of Baptism

2. Being Fully Present: The Grace of Confirmation

3. Giving Oneself Completely: The Grace of the Eucharist

4. Forgiving: The Grace of Reconciliation

5. Healing: The Grace of the Anointing of the Sick

6. Serving: The Grace of Marriage and of Holy Orders

This blueprint is comprised of six attributes of God's love, which have been revealed throughout the history of our salvation and strengthened with the graces of the sacraments.

The attributes of love that anchor this program are inscribed in every person's heart, because we have been created in God's image. This is the type of love we deeply desire. We all want to be accepted, to have commitments, to give and receive, to be forgiven, to be comforted, and to serve or take care of one another. Researchers and psychologists report that these qualities of love are the building blocks of any healthy relationship, and they are especially important in marriage.

Joined by Grace introduces a new paradigm in marriage preparation. Its content is not structured according to common topics, such as finances, sexuality, communication, and sacramentality. Instead, it is structured around an exploration of the seven sacraments, and from each sacrament we draw lessons that address such practical skills as communication, finances, sexuality, sacramentality, spirituality, Natural Family Planning (NFP), and more. This is the aspect of Joined by Grace that is unique in marriage preparation.

Joined by Grace uses an interdisciplinary approach that weaves together three strands of wisdom: the biblical traditions and teachings of the Catholic Church, the best knowledge from leading marriage experts, and the lived experiences of numerous married couples. Faith and science agree about the qualities of love that bring joy and lasting commitment to married couples. These are qualities that we find in Jesus' love for the Church, expressed in the sacraments. They are acceptance, commitment to being present, self-giving, forgiveness, healing, and serving. These qualities are the core of what engaged couples reflect on and learn when using Joined by Grace.

3. We Celebrate with the Engaged Couple

As Jesus did with the disciples on the road to Emmaus, we celebrate with our engaged couples. We read in the Gospel of Luke that Jesus "took bread, said the blessing, broke it, and gave it to them. Then their eyes were opened and they recognized him" (Lk 24:30). We too come to know Jesus better in the breaking of the bread, the Eucharist. Therefore Joined by Grace emphasizes the importance of participation in the Mass for couples during marriage preparation. We encourage mentors to invite the engaged couples to Mass and perhaps meet afterward for coffee or brunch. We urge mentors also to introduce the engaged to other members of the parish so that the couples begin to find support and encouragement in the faith community.

The disciples were changed when they recognized Jesus in the breaking of the bread. Inviting and supporting the efforts of engaged couples to participate in the Mass every Sunday marks the beginning of a gentle process of connecting the couple to the life of the parish that hopefully will continue after the wedding.

4. We Help Engaged Couples Connect with Their Faith Communities

They set out at once and returned to Jerusalem.

—Luke 24:33

As you help millennials connect to parish life, remember that they want to contribute to the community, despite the fact that many of them lead very hectic lives. Jeff Fromm and Christie Garton write in their book *Marketing to Millennials* that millennials want to be engaged in the community and want to participate in what's happening. We need to invite them and give them opportunities to contribute.[6]

Millennials are talented and have a lot to offer. They are tech savvy, most of them are college educated, they have high ideals, they report that making a contribution to society is very important to them, and they want to lead.[7] Yet, many of the couples whom we prepare for marriage disappear after the wedding. We must continually ask ourselves why this is and what changes our parishes can make to help them stay connected and active in the parish.

Very few parishes follow up to stay in touch with them and to invite them to be active parishioners, so they head to other churches or more likely simply find other things that seem more satisfying on Sunday mornings. There are, of course, couples who are married in parishes with no intention of remaining there because they have jobs in other places. It is very likely that if they find a new parish home, no one there is aware of their presence.

Joined by Grace helps parishes find ways to maintain the connections made between engaged couples and the faith community. This is where program directors or coordinators and mentor couples are key. We recommend that all engaged couples, even those who attend a diocesan or regional retreat, be assigned a mentor couple to be their guides and role models during the preparation and into the first months or even years of marriage. More information on this is available in chapters 2 and 4.

The program director or the mentor couple are encouraged to stay in touch with each couple at least once a quarter during the first year and to invite them to social activities or marriage-enrichment events at the parish, as well as to become involved in the parish in such roles as lectors, ushers, parish council committee members, catechists, and so on.

For couples who get married and move away to a different community, we recommend sending a note to the pastor of the parish where the couple is relocating, encouraging that parish community to reach out to this couple and welcome them among their families. A sample note to the new parish is available in chapter 5.

Marriage Preparation Is the Work of the Spirit

Business people and organizations that are successful set goals, track their performances, and measure the results. It is tempting to want to do the same for any marriage-preparation program. However, we have learned that when it comes to parish ministries, such as marriage preparation, it is impossible and dangerous to set expectations in terms of tangible and measurable outcomes. Spiritual progress cannot be measured with human tools, and in setting expectations we may be tempted to take credit for the work of the Holy Spirit. In works of ministry we are only imperfect instruments through which the Holy Spirit works. In this program we dare to set some desired outcomes not because we will measure them but to remind ourselves of what we hope and pray the Holy Spirit will accomplish in the engaged couples and in the parish community through our work.

It is worth asking ourselves: What impact do we expect this program will have on the engaged couples? What change or growth can we expect to see when they finish the program? How will the parish community be enriched by this program? Listed here are our goals for the program. We hope and pray that the Holy Spirit will accomplish many of these through the members of the parish team and the prayers of the whole parish.

Goals of the Program

On their wedding day we expect the bride and the groom to feel

- closer to each other because they have come to know each other better;
- closer to God, having learned that their love story is part of his love story and that Jesus Christ is present in their relationship;
- at home in the Catholic Church because you have helped them find there a community that welcomes them, and a place where they can grow spiritually;

- ready to make a permanent commitment to each other because you have explained and modeled for them the permanence of Christian marriage; and
- ready to accept a role in society as a married couple because they understand that marriage is not a private affair but a relationship in the service of each other, God, and society.

On their wedding day we expect the bride and groom to know

- each other better;
- that marriage is a vocation and is the path to holiness to which they are assenting;
- that Christian married love is modeled after Christ's love for the Church, and it is a sacrament of it;
- that their marital commitment is given freely, is indissoluble, and requires faithfulness;
- that love is self-giving, life-giving, and fruitful;
- that marriages have ups and downs, and it is important to find support in the local faith community;
- that the Catholic view of human sexuality is a positive one;
- that attending Mass regularly and going to confession is beneficial to their relationship;
- that Christ is a partner in their marriage and is ready to help them with his graces; and
- that nurturing and growing their relationship requires many life skills that need to be mindfully practiced, such as communicating effectively, negotiating differences and resolving conflicts peacefully, managing finances together, compromising, forgiving, and sharing household responsibilities.

Impact of the Program on the Parish Community

Through the involvement of the whole parish community as described in chapter 4, the members of the parish:

- will be reminded that marriage is a vocation and a sacrament,

- will come to understand the importance of praying for married couples, and
- will have a heightened awareness that marriage preparation begins in the home.

These outcomes are not something that those ministering to the engaged will achieve on their own. They require the engaged couple's openness to the Holy Spirit and a good deal of work. Prayer will, therefore, be important on the mentors' part, on the part of the engaged couples, and on the part of the whole community.

It is our hope that through prayer, reading, and interacting with the marriage-preparation team, the engaged couples will experience a deepening of their faith, will discover or rediscover the value of the sacraments, feel the love and care of the parish community, and will embrace the power of grace in married life.

The Components of the Program

Joined by Grace has been designed for use in small groups, perhaps one to three engaged couples working with one or two mentor couples. It can also be used in one-on-one settings and can be adapted for a weekend retreat (Friday evening through Saturday or Saturday morning through early Sunday afternoon).

The *Couple's Book*

This book is written in a heart-warming style. It is personal and full of stories from the life of married couples. Each chapter in the *Couple's Book* addresses four topics:

1. What Catholics believe about one of the seven sacraments.
2. What we learn about love from how Christ loves the Church in the sacrament examined in the chapter.
3. The obstacles married couples are likely to encounter.
4. Tools for building a strong marriage. These tools include communication skills and prayers.

The *Mentor Guide*

The *Mentor Guide* provides mentor couples with helpful suggestions for accompanying the engaged couples on their journey to the altar. It shows mentors how to share their faith, their Catholic tradition, and their own experiences of marriage. The *Mentor Guide* provides detailed but flexible outlines for six meetings between engaged couples (in small groups or couple-to-couple encounters) and mentors. It also provides mentor couples with insights about ministering to couples already living together, as well as to interfaith couples, and directs them to online resources that offer more help. The book encourages mentor couples to help engaged couples connect with their parish community through regular Mass attendance, by introducing them to other couples and parish activities, and by following up with them after the wedding.

The *Program Manual*

In this book the program director will find many resources to help you implement this ministry in your parish and adapt the materials to your parish's needs and practices. You will find suggestions and criteria for selecting and recruiting mentor couples, schedules and outlines for training them, and resources for making marriage preparation a ministry of the whole parish. In addition, this manual gives the program director insights on the needs of today's engaged couples.

Joined by Grace DVD with Twenty-Four Short Videos

The resources listed above are supplemented with twenty-four short videos to use during the meetings or a weekend retreat. The videos have been produced by the award-winning Catholic production company Spirit Juice Studios. They feature Catholic married couples who give witness to the joys and struggles of faithfully living out the vocation of Christian marriage and of family life. For each meeting or retreat segment, one video features a pastoral expert who links the graces of our sacraments with building strong, holy marriages.

Program Website

JoinedbyGrace.com contains many resources for mentors and others working in the ministry. Some articles, handouts, and essays are for enrichment or continuing education of mentors themselves, while others are intended to be printed and given to engaged couples or simply drawn to the attention of the engaged couples for reading online.

Some of the many resources found at JoinedbyGrace.com are:

- couple exercises for the six meetings
- retreat outlines
- sample forms and correspondence
- articles on the sacraments
- articles on topics of concern in building strong marriages such as communication skills, finances, NFP, balancing work and home lives, friends, and families
- traditional Catholic prayers
- brief stories of married saints

Scope and Sequence Chart

	MEETING 1	MEETING 2	MEETING 3
Opening prayer	Romans 15 (Welcome one another)	Romans 8 (Christ is always present)	1 John 4 (God is Love)
Video 1	**Marriage Is...**	**Life is Who You're With**	**Always Us, Not Me**
Chapter title	**Welcoming and Accepting**: The Grace and Call of Baptism	**Being Fully Present**: The Grace of Confirmation	**Giving Oneself Completely**: The Grace of the Eucharist
Topic 1: **What Catholics believe about this sacrament, and the graces they receive.**	**Baptism Gives us Graces to Welcome and Accept Each Other** What Catholics believe about Baptism What Baptism teaches us about Marriage How the sacramental graces of Baptism help married couples	**Confirmation Strengthens Us to Be Fully Present** What Catholics believe about Confirmation What Confirmation teaches us about Marriage How the sacramental graces of Confirmation help married couples	**The Eucharist Teaches Us to Give Ourselves Completely** What Catholics believe about the Eucharist What the Eucharist teaches us about Marriage How the sacramental graces of the Eucharist help married couples
Video 2	**The Grace and Call of Baptism**	**The Power of God's Presence**	**The Gift of the Eucharist**
Topic 2: **What we learn about love from how Christ loves the Church in this sacrament.**	**Accepting Your Spouse as Precious Gift** Accepting your spouse as a gift that is different and imperfect Accepting yourself Accepting God's plan for marriage	**Being Present and Attentive to Each Other** Your wedding ring An irrevocable promise The value of commitment and the power of Grace	**Healthy Giving of Oneself** The value of generosity Self-giving and intimacy Chastity in marriage
Video 3	**Choosing to Believe**	**Distractions**	**NFP: Normalizing the Natural**
Topic 3: **The obstacles married couples are likely to encounter**	**Common Obstacles to Accepting Each Other** Unrealistic expectations Other obstacles • Roles learned from family • Poor communication skills • Habits of independent life • Low self-esteem	**Common Obstacles to Being Fully Present** Special friends Social networks Use of pornography	**Common Obstacles to Giving Oneself Completely** Selfishness
Video 4	**It's the Little Things**	**Money**	**Mass: The Training Ground**
Topic 4: **Tools for building a strong marriage**	**Communication** Listening and accepting advice Skills in effective listening **Prayer** Praying for mutual acceptance Serenity Prayer	**Communication** Making a budget Managing your money Expressing yourself clearly **Prayer** Remembering that God is always present Developing prayer habits Praying the Glory Be	**Communication** A conflict resolution method **Prayer** Participate in the Eucharist regularly
Closing prayer	A Blessing for the engaged	Prayer to the Holy Spirit by St. Augustine	The Our Father
Lives of married saints (available online)	Mary and Joseph	Blessed Luigi and Maria Quattrocchi	St. Gianna Molla

MEETING 4	MEETING 5	MEETING 6
1 Corinthians 13 (If I do not have love, I gain nothing)	Psalm 145 (The Lord is compassionate)	Romans 12 (Serve the Lord)
Everyone Needs Forgiveness	**Rooted in Prayer**	**Joined to Serve**
Forgiving: The Grace of Reconciliation	**Healing:** the Grace of the Anointing of the Sick	**Serving**: The Grace of Marriage and Holy Orders
The Sacrament of Reconciliation Frees Us to Forgive What Catholics believe about the sacrament of Reconciliation What Reconciliation teaches us about Marriage How the sacramental graces of Reconciliation help married couples	**The Sacrament of Anointing Brings Us Healing** What Catholics believe about the Sacrament of Anointing of the Sick What Anointing of the Sick teaches us about Marriage How the sacramental graces of Anointing of the Sick help married couples	**The Sacraments of Marriage and Holy Orders Call Us to Serve** What Catholics believe about Marriage and Holy Orders What the sacraments of Service teach us about Marriage How sacramental grace of Marriage helps married couples
The Grace of Reconciliation	**God's Healing Grace**	**Sacramental Calling**
Learning to Forgive Unconditionally Forgiveness is a decision Admitting your faults Reconciliation	**Learning to Bring Comfort and Healing** Make your relationship your priority The need for compassion His needs, her needs	**Serving Each Other and Together Serving God** Listen to your call The call to serve as parents God is the creator of life Natural Family Planning
The Gift and the Challenge	**When Sorrow Comes**	**Kids**
Common Obstacles to Forgiving and Reconciling Anger and resentment Avoid the Four Horsemen	**Common Obstacles to Comfort and Healing** Denial	**Common Obstacles to Serving with Love** The influence of secular individualism How do we stay on course?
Beyond Conflict	**Work and Marriage**	**Families, Friends, and Role Models**
Communication The problem of venting your frustrations with friends How to ask forgiveness **Prayer** Examination of conscience Going to confession	**Communication** Attitudes make a difference Divorce is not the answer The value of suffering The power of physical touch **Prayer** Why Catholics pray to Mary Hail Mary / Rosary	**Communication** Manage the use of electronic tools Sharing meals together as a couple and as a family **Prayer** Prayer of gratitude Prayer before meals
The Act of Contrition	Prayer of St. Francis	Pray the Hail Mary
Sts. Louis and Zélie Martin	St. Rita of Cascia	St. Elizabeth Ann Seton

2.

Implementing the Program in Your Parish

Getting Started

Here are simple steps you can take to get started. Some of these are things that you may be doing if you already have a well-established marriage-preparation ministry in your parish.

Become Familiar with Joined by Grace

Read the *Couple's Book* and the *Mentor Guide* and watch the videos as you see them listed in the meeting outlines. Explore the supporting materials available to you at JoinedbyGrace.com and TogetherforLifeOnline.com.

If a decision has already been made to use Joined by Grace, skip to "Identify Potential Mentor Couples."

If a decision has not yet been made to use this program, ask yourself the following questions, or if possible, gather a small group of interested parishioners to discuss these with you.

- Does this program help us implement the diocesan marriage-preparation policy?
- If we are currently using a different marriage-preparation program, how does Joined by Grace compare with the present program with regard to the content, the approach, and the tools needed to implement it?
- If we were to use Joined by Grace, what would we have to do differently from what we are doing today?
- Who would coordinate the activities of this program?
- Does Joined by Grace meet the expectations of our pastor for a marriage-preparation program?
- Do we know married couples who can serve as mentor couples?
- How can we ask the whole community to pray for those called to the vocation of marriage and those preparing for it?

Having answered the questions above, you are ready to approach the pastor, parish council, or the person(s) who will make the decision about adopting the program.

Talk with the Key Decision Makers

For this program to be effectively implemented, you will need the agreement and the support of the pastor and others in the parish who have a leadership role. The decision makers may depend on you to present the benefits of this program. Your answers to the questions you explored above will help you to be ready for this meeting.

The agreement and support of the pastor is needed because canon law tells us that the pastor is responsible for the care of marriages and families in the parish, including the preparation for marriage.[1] More information on the role of clergy in marriage preparation is presented in the next section, "The Marriage-Preparation Team."

Decide Which Format Is Best for Your Parish

In your meeting with the pastor or other decision makers, discuss and agree on the format of the program that is best for your parish. Joined by Grace is designed to be used in small groups or couple-to-couple settings. There are two weekend retreat sample adaptations available at JoinedbyGrace.com. Often parishes will need both the meeting and the retreat models in order to accommodate couples who live in separate cities or are traveling back to a home parish for marriage preparation and their wedding. Find a description of these formats in "Using the Program in Different Formats," on page 27.

Identify Potential Mentor Couples

Having obtained the agreement of the pastor and the decision makers to use Joined by Grace, and having determined the format desired for your parish (small group or retreat), you can now discuss and plan for the implementation process. One of the first tasks will be to identify couples in your parish that you believe will be good mentors. If your parish already has a marriage-preparation program, you probably have a team of couples who may be willing to take on this role. If you need to recruit mentor couples, make a list of couples you want to invite to the ministry. Do this together with your pastor and other interested people who know the parish well. You can read more about the criteria for selecting mentor couples in chapter 3, page 33.

Invite Couples to the Ministry

The pastor, or his delegate who is responsible for coordinating marriage preparation, should then extend an invitation to those you have identified as potential mentor couples. Make this invitation through a letter, e-mail, phone call, or in person. If the initial outreach goes out via letter or e-mail, be certain to ask if you may contact the potential mentor couple by phone or in person to chat more about the program. Explain briefly what the program requires of the mentor couple, and assure them that they will receive training and have access to ongoing support. Without asking for a commitment, invite them to attend an informational meeting during which you will explain the program and the role of the mentor couple. Be mindful of choosing a time for the meeting that seems convenient to most. You may even list a few options and have two or more meetings to accommodate varied schedules, especially if you have a large parish with many weddings.

Schedule and Hold an Informational Meeting

Set a date for a short informational meeting (either one hour or one and a half hours), and send a written invitation to all the couples you would like to become involved in your parish's marriage-preparation ministry using Joined by Grace. If a lot of time has elapsed from the date of the initial invitation, you may want to follow the meeting invitation with a phone call. A sample invitation is available in chapter 5, page 64.

The purpose of this meeting is not to train the volunteers in their role as mentor couples but to explain what the ministry is about, answer questions, ascertain their desire to serve in this role, and obtain their commitment. See a sample agenda for this meeting in chapter 3, page 36.

Hold a Training Meeting

Once you have the commitment from a sufficient number of couples, hold a training meeting. This could be held on a weekend and can last two to four hours, depending on the needs of your team. Find a detailed agenda for this training in chapter 3, page 38.

Launch the Program

Having completed the training of your mentor couples, you are ready to introduce the ministry of marriage preparation using Joined by Grace to your parish.

- During a Sunday Mass, hold a commissioning ceremony for all mentor couples. Make this a public event, during which time the pastor or you can explain to the parish the Church's commitment to supporting marriages and to preparing couples for marriage. This commissioning could be repeated annually, perhaps during the annual National Marriage Week. Find a sample commissioning ceremony in chapter 4, page 53.
- Use the parish website, bulletin, or newsletter to educate the parish community about the importance of the marriage vocation to the Church. Use the quotations provided in "Parish Bulletin Announcements" found at JoinedbyGrace.com.
- Recruit a volunteer minister with good organizational skills and an inviting personality to organize a "prayer partners" ministry. This is a structured way for parishioners to

support the engaged couples through prayer. Find more information about how to do this in chapter 4.

- Publish articles on marriage on the parish website or in your bulletin or newsletter. Invite guest speakers, or offer retreats focused on spiritual issues crucial to healthy, holy marriages.
- List the names of the couples preparing for marriage in the parish bulletin, and invite the members of the parish to pray for them during this special time and in the future.
- Regularly add petitions to the Universal Prayer at weekend Masses for those preparing for marriage, for those who are married, and especially for those who struggle with living their vocation.

The Marriage-Preparation Team

Earlier we stated that marriage preparation is a ministry of accompaniment. In every parish there is a team of people who come in contact with the engaged couple and accompany them. Each has a different role, and sometimes one person carries more than one role. Often, some of these do not realize that they are active in this ministry.

The First Point of Contact

The first team member is often the parish secretary or the person who answers the phone when an engaged couple calls inquiring about getting married at the church. This person has an important role in this ministry. From the way the phone is answered, to the information given, to the tone of voice, the approach of the first point of contact represents to the engaged couple the attitudes of the Church toward them and toward their preparation for the sacrament of Marriage.

Speaking to pastors and pastoral workers in his diocese, Pope Francis emphasized that it is important for pastors to surround themselves with people who have a welcoming attitude, especially the church secretaries. He said that parish secretaries open the front door of the mother's home [the Church] with welcome and tenderness.

The Priest or Deacon

The priest or deacon plays a central role in marriage preparation and in the wedding celebration because of what the Church expects the pastor or his delegates to do. The role of the pastor is clearly defined by the *Code of Canon Law*: "Pastors of souls are obliged to ensure that their own church community provides for Christ's faithful the assistance by which the married state is preserved in its Christian character and develops in perfection."[2] Pastors are to ensure that their own parish assists those married and those preparing for marriage. This assistance is to be given through their preaching and instructions, by personal preparation of those entering marriage, and "by the fruitful celebration of the marriage liturgy." In addition, canon 1066 states that the role of the priest in marriage preparation is to establish that "nothing stands in the way of its valid and [lawful] celebration."[3]

Often, when engaged couples come to the parish to meet with the priest or deacon, it may be the first time that they have spoken personally with a member of the clergy. This, as we mentioned earlier, is both an opportunity and a challenge. While the couple may come asking for a wedding, the role of the pastor is to assess the spiritual needs of the engaged couple and to redirect their expectations from planning the wedding to preparing for marriage.

Fr. Jay Biber expresses these thoughts in a paper published by the USCCB: "The Role of Clergy in Marriage Preparation." He writes that today many couples come to the parish asking for marriage "more or less un-evangelized." They are often unaware not only of Church teachings about marriage but also of the core notions of the Catholic faith and the basic practices of the faith. Fr. Biber writes that the presence of the priest or deacon in marriage preparation is an opportunity for evaluating the couple's needs and setting in place a plan that leads to marriage preparation rather than just wedding preparation.[4]

Pope Benedict XVI expressed a similar thought in his address in 2011 to the Roman Rota (the highest Church tribunal). He said that a tool for ascertaining a couple's right intentions and freedom to marry is the premarital examination. While the primary purpose of this examination is mainly juridical, it should not be treated as a bureaucratic step. "Instead it is a unique pastoral opportunity . . . in which, through a dialogue full of respect and cordiality, the pastor seeks to help the person to face seriously the truth about himself or herself and about his or her own human and Christian vocation for marriage."[5]

Today, pastors and priests often feel overwhelmed by the many needs of their parish community. Because of this, pastors surround themselves with well-trained and capable helpers to whom they delegate certain tasks in the marriage-preparation process.

Some permanent deacons have been called to fill some of these tasks. The work of the marriage-preparation program director and the mentor couples in a parish are extensions of the work of the pastor.

While the work of lay volunteers is important in preparing couples for marriage, it cannot replace the value and the impact of a priest's presence and active involvement in the preparation process. To engaged couples, the priest represents the Church more than anyone else in the parish.

The Program Director

The program director or coordinator is responsible for ensuring that the process runs smoothly. Doing so relieves the pastor or his delegate from worrying about some of the administrative details that the program demands.

While the responsibilities of the program director may differ from parish to parish, common responsibilities include the following:

- Receiving or responding to the first call from engaged couples asking to be married in the parish. The program director can be the person whose name and phone number are associated with marriage preparation on the parish website or in the parish bulletin.
- Scheduling the first meeting of the engaged couple with the priest or deacon.
- Assisting the pastor or his delegate in recruiting mentor couples.
- Coordinating the training of mentor couples.
- Scheduling a commissioning of mentor couples.
- Ordering Joined by Grace materials as needed.
- Linking engaged couples with mentor couples or small groups.
- Planning and directing or overseeing weekend retreats if that format is used.
- Overseeing a network of prayer partners.
- Reviewing program evaluations submitted by the engaged couples and implementing improvements as needed.

- Staying in contact with engaged couples through all stages of their preparation and in the future.
- Creating bulletin announcements to invite the whole parish to pray for the engaged.
- Coordinating ongoing education of the parish by placing marriage quotations in the bulletin. These are available at JoinedbyGrace.com.

The director or coordinator of marriage preparation should be a staff member or volunteer who has the skills both to see the big picture and to think systematically about how to implement the program. The person needs to be organized and also be skilled at discerning in others the gifts needed to become good mentors or to help in other aspects of the ministry.

Among the tools available in this manual and at JoinedbyGrace.com to assist the program director are the following:

- Sample welcome letters to the engaged couples and to the mentor couples, found in chapter 5.
- Tips on recruiting mentor couples and an outline for their training in chapter 3.
- Materials for a "Marriage Matters" campaign using space in the parish bulletin, found in chapter 4.
- Additional resources, found in chapter 5.

The Mentor Couple

These couples are role models for the engaged. They are people of faith who are willing to share with engaged couples lessons learned in the years of their marriages. During the time spent with the mentor couples, those preparing for marriage will see Christian husbands and wives interact with each other, help each other, and even disagree with each other. The engaged couples will learn from them what Christian married life is about. The mentor couples should be encouraged to remain in contact with the couples they mentor through the first months of marriage and hopefully longer.

To avoid intruding in the family life of the mentor couple, we recommend that these couples be expected to mentor a small group of engaged couples no more than once a year. These small groups may be composed of two or three engaged couples or only one. Being a mentor couple is a commitment of time and effort that involves the whole family and hopefully continues after the wedding. Not all families can commit to mentoring more than once a year. Use this information as a guide to help you decide how many mentor couples to recruit in your parish.

We recommend assigning a mentor couple to all those who enter the marriage-preparation process, whether the parish uses the small-group format or the retreat format. When a parish sends an engaged couple to a regional or diocesan retreat, there is a danger that the engaged couple perceives the marriage-preparation process as something disconnected from the parish community. The role of the mentor couple in these cases may include the following:

- Making contact by phone or e-mail with the engaged couple to introduce themselves and explain their role.
- Praying for the engaged couple assigned to them.
- During the weeks or months of engagement, trying to attend the Sunday Mass that the engaged couple is attending.
- Getting to know the couple over lunch or dinner.
- After the wedding, staying in touch with the young married couple.
- If the newlyweds are living in the community, inviting them to attend social events, and spiritual or educational functions at the parish.
- Introducing the young couple to other young couples in the parish.

Use the above list to brainstorm ways in which the parish can provide every engaged couple with a mentor to accompany them during their engagement and in the future.

The Wedding Planner

The wedding planner helps the engaged couple prepare for wedding celebrations. He or she has a role to play in keeping the couple focused on the spiritual meaning of this event. Pope Francis's advice to engaged couples is that "it is good that your wedding be simple and make what is truly important stand out. Some are more concerned with the exterior details, with the banquet, the photographs, the clothes, the flowers. . . . These are important for a celebration, but only if they point to the real reason for your joy: the Lord's blessing on your love."[6]

It is important that the wedding planner understand the spirit of Joined by Grace so as to convey that same spirit to the engaged couples in support of the efforts of the marriage-preparation team. To this end, it is recommended that the wedding planner be included in some of the training received by the rest of the marriage-preparation team.

The Whole Parish Community

The last but not least among the team members is the whole faith community: the parish. Pope Francis writes in *Amoris Laetitia*: "The complexity of today's society and the challenges faced by the family require a greater effort on the part of the whole Christian community in preparing those who are about to be married" (206). We encourage parishes to accompany the engaged couples as a community. When a couple comes to the parish and asks to be married in the Church, they may be thinking that their wedding is a private event. The persons accompanying them need to emphasize that getting married is a community event, and their parish is happy for them and is praying for them.

The strongest support a parish community can offer couples preparing for marriage is prayer. Therefore, invite individual parish members, couples, and especially families to become prayer partners to the engaged couples participating in Joined by Grace. Assign to them a couple who is preparing for marriage. The commitment of the prayer partners will be to pray each day for the engaged couple until the day of the wedding and beyond. Encourage prayer partners to write to the engaged couple, telling them that they are praying for them. Invite them also to stay in contact with the couple after the wedding, if they feel comfortable doing so. The program director may act as a go–between in this communication, or with the permission of the engage couple, give their address to the prayer partners. Receiving a letter or an e-mail from someone praying for them during a difficult moment may be a ray of sunshine the couple needs to help them get past the challenge. In chapter 5 you will find a sample note you can use to assign engaged couples to the prayer partners.

Using the Program in Different Formats

Dioceses and parishes approach marriage preparation in different ways. The approaches vary depending on the needs and number of engaged couples and the ability of the diocese or parish to have trained personnel to mentor the engaged. In this program we will organize the materials into two formats that are common across the United States.

The Small-Group or Couple-to-Couple Format

- The small-group format provides an ideal setting for the mentor couple to develop a relationship with the engaged and connect them to the life of the parish. Some engaged people will be more comfortable working with other engaged couples than working one-on-one with the mentor couple. Conversation may be easier or harder, depending on the makeup of the group. Other engaged couples will benefit more from couple-to-couple ministry. Of course, the availability of mentor couples will play a large role in deciding how to organize the program. Give all of this careful thought, and develop a system that helps you determine what is best for your setting and for each engaged couple.
- If you opt for small groups, the size of the group can vary from one engaged couple to three, and you might consider one or two mentors. Much larger than this size can make substantive conversation difficult. Be creative, and carefully assess your needs, strengths, and weaknesses.
- The marriage-preparation process of Joined by Grace is designed to unfold over the course of six meetings. An introductory meeting, perhaps with a meal, might be helpful in simply getting everyone introduced to each other and the program. Likewise, a wrap-up meeting or potluck dinner is a good idea in some situations.
- Meetings can take place on parish property or—preferably—in mentors' homes. Another option is to create a ministry of hospitality through which families or other parishioners can host these meetings in their homes without also be asked to act as mentors. These parishioners would simply provide a welcoming, clean place for groups to meet, perhaps along with light refreshments. This helps not only to disperse

responsibilities, but it encourages more people to be consistently mindful of this important ministry of the Church.

- Each meeting is scheduled to last between two hours and two and a half hours—about the length of a movie.
- A detailed outline for each meeting is available in the *Mentor Guide*.
- During the meeting, the mentor couple strives to keep a balance between input on Church teaching and relationship skills, their own personal sharing, private time for the engaged couples to talk together, and group conversations. Four videos assigned for each meeting are interspersed with other conversation; they function as conversation starters rather than deliverers of all the doctrinal core of the program, as you will find in some other programs.
- Engaged couples should come to meetings having read the corresponding chapter in the *Couple's Book* and reflected on the questions of that chapter.

The Weekend Retreat Adaption

- The adaption to a weekend retreat is available at JoinedbyGrace.com. This format is especially useful for couples who live in different cities or states and cannot attend weekly meetings together. It is also helpful for couples in which one or both travel a lot during the week and are home on weekends.
- Diocesan or parish leaders can easily adapt the schedule suggested at JoinedbyGrace.com and briefly described here in chapter 3 to meet local needs.
- The retreat is broken up into sessions of one and a half to two hours each with ample time for meals, socializing, and private reflection.
- Each session will include time for input, couple private reflection, and group sharing.
- The weekend retreat should be held in a facility where couples can be housed for the night; a retreat center is ideal. It can also be held at the parish or at some other facility without providing overnight accommodations. In this case, the engaged couples go home for the night and return the next day to continue the program. When using this option, the program can be less expensive while still offering a rich experience.

- The retreat is led by a team of couples and individuals responsible for a variety of tasks, from greeting and welcoming attendees, to facilitating the meetings, to cooking (if necessary), and so on. The retreat format is likely to be more effective when a lead couple has been assigned to coordinate all the activities and to act as directors throughout the event. It is crucial to separate the hospitality tasks from those of directing the sessions between different people, unless the group is very small.

The Overall Parish Program Timeline

The following is a suggested timeline for the program's activities in a parish during the preparation process and after the wedding. It is important, however, that each parish develop its own timeline, one that works best for the community. Be creative and strategic in your planning!

The schedule that follows assumes that the engaged couple contacts the parish at least six months before the wedding. When that does not happen, the timeline will need to be shortened. It also assumes that a marriage-preparation program, either in the weekend retreat or the small-group format, will be offered once a quarter in the parish or the region.

Week 1

The process starts when the couple calls to make an appointment. The program director welcomes them and helps them schedule a meeting with the priest or deacon who will work with them during the period of preparation.

Weeks 2 and 3

The priest or deacon begins a series of meetings with the engaged couple according to the requirements of the diocesan policy.

The program director assigns the couple to a mentor couple leading a small group or to a weekend retreat with a mentor couple to accompany them leading up to and following that retreat.

Week 4

A welcoming letter is sent to the engaged couple either by the program director or by the mentor couple to invite them to the marriage-preparation program and to introduce them to the mentor couple.

If the couple will be attending the weekend retreat, the letter will give them directions to the location and will specify what they can do to prepare for the retreat.

In chapter 5 sample letters are provided for couples attending a small-group marriage-preparation program and for couples attending a marriage-preparation retreat.

Week 5

The priest or deacon continues meetings with the engaged couple.

Week 6

The mentor couple contacts the engaged couple by phone and reminds them of the dates for the small-group meetings and location.

If the couple has been assigned to a weekend retreat, a member of the retreat team will call them to welcome them, confirm their attendance, and answer questions they may have.

Week 7

The priest or deacon continues meetings with the engaged couple.

Week 8

A blessing of engaged couples is celebrated at the parish using the Order for Blessing of an Engaged Couple from the revised *Order of Celebrating Matrimony*.

The retreat is held.

Couple-to-couple or small-group meetings begin with

Meeting 1: Welcoming and Accepting: The Grace and Call of Baptism

Week 9

Meeting 2: Being Fully Present: The Grace of Confirmation

Week 10

Meeting 3: Giving Oneself Completely: The Grace of the Eucharist

Week 11

Meeting 4: Forgiving: The Grace of Reconciliation

Week 12

Meeting 5: Healing: The Grace of the Anointing of the Sick

Week 13

Meeting 6: Serving: The Grace of Marriage and of Holy Orders

Weeks 14, 15, 16, and following

The priest or deacon continues and concludes meetings with the engaged couple.

Weeks 17, 18, 19, and 20

The engaged couple meets with the parish wedding planner to understand the parish requirements and guidelines for the wedding activities during the celebration of the *Order of Celebrating Matrimony.*

Wedding Day

Staying in Contact

It is important that, after the wedding, the parish remain in contact with the newly married couples.

Approaching the Wedding

- The program director may develop a database or use the parish database to keep important information on all the couples going through the program. In it he or she will collect at least the couples' names, e-mail addresses, and telephone numbers.
- If while speaking with a couple, the priest, the mentor couple, or the program director become aware that after the wedding the newlyweds are planning to move to a different part of the city or to a different town, ask the couple if it is okay for the parish

to continue to stay in touch. Inform the couple that the parish will send a note to their new pastor to introduce them to him. (See the sample note in chapter 5.)

Three Months Follow-Up

- The mentor couple, the program director, or a pastoral minister sends a personal note to the couple wishing them well. This could also be a phone call.

Six Months Follow-Up

- The program director or someone involved in parish ministries contacts the couple to invite them to become active in one of the parish ministries. In addition, the mentor couple invites the newlyweds to dinner.

One Year Follow-Up

- The parish can send an anniversary card to the newlyweds. Consider asking a volunteer to take on this task. Often in parishes there are those who enjoy such responsibilities that they can do from home.
- The program director, with the help of some of the mentor couples, can plan a date-night event for the newly married couples in the parish or in the region.

Activities throughout the Year

- The program director can use the information collected in his or her database to stay in contact with newly married couples. For example, he or she can send from time to time inspirational articles on marriage, or newsletters for newly married couples.
- A list of resources and programs that can be helpful to newly married couples appears in chapter 4, and many resources are available at JoinedbyGrace.com.

3.

Recruiting and Training Mentor Couples

You may already have a marriage-preparation program in existence and a sufficient number of mentor couples whom you can train to use this program. Even if that is the case, you may find the information in this chapter helpful in evaluating your current program. If, on the other hand, you are blessed and happy with a well-functioning mentor ministry structure, skip ahead to the next chapter.

The recruitment and selection process for members of the marriage-preparation team is best done with the assistance of the pastor, or the priest or deacon delegated by him. Often the pastor or members of the clergy know couples in the parish that can make a valuable contribution to this ministry.

Recruiting Mentor Couples and Criteria for Selection

Keep in mind that you are not looking for perfect couples. Those do not exist. The couples whom you want are those that, to the best of your and the pastor's knowledge:

- practice their faith;

- are willing to share their faith and their marriage with others;
- recognize their own imperfections, and in spite of their own shortcomings are striving to grow together; and
- would like to help others.

There are other critical criteria that the pastor will certainly keep in mind.

- The couple needs to be in a valid marriage recognized by the Church.
- The couple should be committed to the Church and its teachings.

The Pontifical Council for the Family gives some general guidelines for the selection of pastoral workers for ministry to engaged couples. The document describes those who work with engaged couples as follows:

- They are persons who have a "solid doctrinal preparation and unquestionable fidelity to the Magisterium of the Church so that they will be able to transmit the truths of the faith and the responsibilities connected with marriage."
- They are persons who are capable of welcoming the engaged regardless of their social background.
- "Based on their own experiences in life and human problems, they can offer some starting points for enlightening the engaged with Christian wisdom."[1]

Together with the pastor or his designate, decide how many mentor couples you want to recruit and train. This will depend on the number of weddings that take place in your parish in a given year. Remember, we suggest that mentors only mentor once a year. This may, however, mean that they work with one, two, or three engaged couples if you are using small groups. A medium-sized parish with about a dozen weddings a year, for example, may need to run a small group once a quarter. These groups may vary from one engaged couple to three, depending on the time of the year and the size of the parish.

Together with the pastor or his representative, develop a list of couples whom the pastor would trust with this responsibility. These are couples you believe will be effective in sharing their experience of marriage, both the good times and the difficult ones, and that meet the criteria listed above. It is also good to expose engaged couples to those who have children at home. If the meetings are held in a home, observing the interactions between the parents and children will be beneficial to the engaged couples.

Agree together on who should approach these potential mentor couples and how. For example, the priest or the deacon may see them at daily or Sunday Mass. Making a personal contact with them is always preferable to a contact by phone. But in some cases a phone call may be necessary.

Some parishes recruit members of the marriage-preparation team using the parish bulletin. This is obviously an approach that can bring quick results; however, a downside to this approach is that you or the pastor may not know all the couples coming forward and volunteering through this type of appeal. It will require time and effort to get to know them. On the positive side, an open invitation to serve in this ministry made through the parish bulletin offers an opportunity to those couples who are not presently involved in the parish or are new to the parish. If the parish uses the bulletin to recruit members of the marriage-preparation team, it is essential that you or the priest or deacon visit personally with each of the couples who volunteers. You can then decide whether they are suited to this ministry and either invite them to the training or direct them toward a different ministry in the parish.

Holding an Informational Meeting

When introducing Joined by Grace, invite all members of the team and any new recruits to an informational meeting. The purpose of this meeting is not to train the couples but to inform them about the program, introduce the new members, ascertain their desire to serve in this ministry, and obtain their commitment. At the end of the meeting, if any of the couples feel they are not called to this ministry or need to wait for a better time, thank them for coming and ask them to be in touch with you if something changes affecting their discernment. For those who have been members of the marriage-preparation team for a while and no longer feel called, be sure to thank them for their past service.

Keep the meeting short, not longer than one hour or at most one and a half hours. If possible, provide child care. Consider meeting over a meal, especially if most couples have busy work schedules. Following is a sample agenda. You can draw the materials for your presentations from different parts of this manual and the other materials of Joined by Grace. To give those present a taste of the tone and spirit of the program, you may also show video clips.

Sample Agenda for the Informational Meeting

1. Begin with a brief opening prayer and an introduction of the current members of the team. Then introduce the new couples who are considering this ministry.
2. Stress the importance of this ministry to the Church. Draw on the information you read in chapter 1 of this manual. You might also review section 66 of *Familiaris Consortio* by St. John Paul II and Pope Francis's *Amoris Laetitia*, especially chapter 6, for insight and quotations to underscore what you present.
3. Explain the reason the parish is using Joined by Grace. Use this as an opportunity to clarify in your own words what you find compelling about the program as a great fit for your parish. Present a list of solid reasons why you and your pastor have chosen this approach to marriage preparation.
4. During this informational meeting, circulate copies of the *Couple's Book* and *Mentor Guide* and view at least the program trailer available at JoinedbyGrace.com and possibly some of the meeting videos. Also preview some of the other offerings at JoinedbyGrace.com, either by looking at them together if you have tech support to do this, or by sharing a list of some of the supporting materials available there.
5. Explain how Joined by Grace will be implemented: the format you will use in your parish.
6. Explain also that this will be a community effort; for example, the parish at large will be asked to pray for the engaged couples and for those who prepare them for marriage. Describe the "prayer partner" ministry if you are beginning one.
7. Inform those present of their role: what will be expected of them, where the meetings will be held, and how often they will meet.
8. Answer any questions they may have.
9. Close the meeting by inviting each couple to commit to serving the Church in this ministry. Explain that your goal is to ask mentor couples to lead a small group or

a weekend retreat no more than once a year. Give the group a date by which you would like their answers, and assure them that you will be praying as they discern whether they are called to this ministry at this time.

10. Announce the date of the upcoming training, making sure that the commitment date mentioned above is at least two weeks prior to training. For any couples ready to commit, supply them with a Mentor Pack, which contains two each of the *Couple's Book* and *Mentor Guide*, as well as the Joined by Grace DVD. Each mentor will need his or her own books so that each person can make notes during planning and preparation and be able to use the books as needed during meetings or retreat sessions.

The Training of Mentor Couples

The effectiveness of Joined by Grace will depend greatly on the way the mentor couples embrace their role as fellow travelers and mentors; on their ability to share the message of the program and illustrate it with examples from their own lives; and on their courage to share how their faith has helped them in their marriage. While the right selection of the mentor couples is critical to the success of the program, a key factor in its effectiveness is the training that the mentor couples receive.

Joined by Grace has been designed so that it is easy to implement and requires minimal training. However, it is important that the program director properly introduce program materials and format to the marriage-preparation team.

This training meeting should involve the key members of the marriage-preparation team. This includes the priests and the deacons who prepare the engaged couples for marriage. It will also be beneficial to include the person who will usually be the first point of contact, as well as the wedding planner, in at least the overview of the program, including its vision and goals. The more all the members of the team are aware of the spirit of the program and of one another's roles, the better the parish can serve the engaged couples.

Two or three hours should be enough time to present a solid introduction to the program and briefly to explore each component. It will be helpful to ask those who will attend to read the introductory portions of both the *Couple's Book* and the *Mentor Guide*.

Agenda for the Training Meeting

Ideally the training is led by the program director together with the priest or deacon who is responsible for the marriage preparation in the parish. As mentioned earlier, mentor couples attending the training should come to the meeting having read at least the front matter of both the *Couple's Book* and the *Mentor Guide*.

I. Welcome and Opening Prayer	10 minutes
II. Introduction to the Program	20 minutes
1. What Is Unique about Joined by Grace?	
2. The Message and Theological Background	
3. The Tools	
III. How the Program Will Be Used in Our Parish	10 minutes
1. The Format to Be Used	
2. The Small-Group Format	
3. The Weekend Retreat Format	
4. The Roles of the Marriage-Preparation Team Members	
IV. Tips for Facilitation	10 minutes
V. Time for Reflection and Practice	60 to 120 minutes
VI. Closing	10 minutes
1. You Are Not Alone	
2. The Role of the Holy Spirit	

I. Welcome and Opening Prayer

Welcome all participants and thank them for their commitment to this ministry. Review the schedule for the training, and if some are not familiar with the building where the training is held, give them directions to the facilities and refreshments.

We suggest the use of one of the prayers provided in the *Mentor Guide*. They are found at the beginning of each meeting in the small-group format. The purpose of this is to give the mentor couples the experience of how you would like the opening prayer for each session to be led. These prayers include readings from scripture passages used at Catholic weddings.

II. Introduction to the Program

Here are some talking points. This introduction can be given by the program director or by the priest or deacon who are members of the team. In this introduction you may want to repeat some of the key points presented during the informational meeting, such as the importance of marriage preparation to the life of the Church and the reason the parish is using Joined by Grace.

1. What Is Unique about Joined by Grace?

This program is unique because the *Couple's Book* is more than a workbook. The *Couple's Book*, together with the twenty-four videos, delivers the content of the program. One of the benefits of this is that the subjects to be addressed are clearly presented in the *Couple's Book* and in the videos. Therefore, the mentor couples do not have to research the subjects on their own. In addition, the topics are supplemented with online articles and tools at JoinedbyGrace.com for mentor couples to use.

Like most marriage-preparation programs, Joined by Grace addresses topics such as communications, finances, sexuality, and spirituality. However, these are not presented as standalone subjects. They are addressed throughout the chapters of the *Couple's Book* and the videos. The program does so because married life is never compartmentalized. The overarching theme that connects all aspects of married life is love, the love of Jesus for the Church, which spouses are called to imitate.

Throughout the chapters of the *Couple's Book*, the program weaves the wisdom of the Catholic tradition, the findings of marriage and family experts, and the lessons learned by married couples. Another unique quality of this program is that it teaches through stories. Each chapter in the *Couple's Book* has at least four anecdotes drawn from the lives of married couples.

The primary purpose of the program is to help the engaged couples understand that they are called to be a sacrament. They do so by loving each other as Jesus loves the

Church. The program identifies the love of Christ for the Church, as expressed in the seven sacraments of the Catholic Church, as a blueprint engaged couples are to use in building their marriage. The program materials seek to assure engaged couples that the graces of the Church's sacraments are available to them to strengthen them as individuals and as spouses.

2. The Message and Theological Background

The main message of the program is that marital happiness flows from personal holiness, and spouses grow in holiness when they learn to love each other as Jesus loves. The theological background of Joined by Grace reflects the teachings of the Catholic Church from Vatican II to Pope Francis. You can find other relevant points on this subject in the "Program Overview" in the *Couple's Book* and in the "Program Structure" in the *Mentor Guide*.

3. The Tools

Be sure to introduce and explain to the marriage-preparation team the components of the program that will be used: the *Couple's Book*, *Mentor Guide*, videos, online articles, and other materials. No other materials should be used by the mentors without first discussing these with the program director.

III. How the Program Will Be Used in Our Parish

1. The Format to Be Used

Explain how the parish plans to use the program; in other words, will the parish use the small-group format or the weekend retreat format? Give a brief explanation of the one you will use.

2. The Small-Group Format

All the sessions have a similar format and roughly coincide with the chapters of the *Couple's Book*.

a) Welcome and Opening Prayer

b) Personal Introductions (necessary only at the first meetings)

c) Introduction of the Topic for the Meeting

d) What Catholics Believe about the Sacraments

e) What the Sacraments Teach Us about Marriage

f) Obstacles Married Couples Are Likely to Encounter

g) Discussion about Tools for Building a Strong Marriage

h) Closing Comments and Prayer

Use the "Meeting at a Glance" chart from the *Mentor Guide* to illustrate how each meeting with the engaged will be structured.

Explain that there is always going to be more material than time. Mentor couples should use the material that they think is most valuable for the engaged couples they are mentoring.

3. The Weekend Retreat Format

Although the materials and the subjects to be covered during the weekend retreat are the same as in the small group, the format is slightly different due to the limited amount of time.

The retreat is composed of six sessions. Each session begins with all the couples gathered as one group for an opening presentation. This will last approximately thirty-five minutes.

Then participants divide into small groups, each facilitated by a mentor couple. This will last approximately forty minutes. During this time the following activities will take place:

a) Processing What Has Been Presented in the General Session

b) Time for Personal Reflection

c) Time for Couple Sharing

d) Time for Group Sharing

4. The Roles of the Marriage-Preparation Team Members

Explain the role of the priest or deacon; the program director; the mentor couple, and how often they can be expected to be called on to lead a group or a retreat; the wedding planner; and the first point of contact. See the role descriptions in the chapter 2 subsection, "The Marriage-Preparation Team" (p. 21).

IV. Tips for Facilitation

The skills required in facilitating meetings in the small-group format or the weekend retreat sessions can be learned. Unfortunately, the time available during this training for mentor couples is very limited. Following are some tips that the program director can encourage mentor couples to keep in mind. The director should feel free to add what he or she has found effective in his or her own experience.

Regardless of which format the parish is using, the mentor couple will be involved in several types of interactions with the engaged couples. Each requires a different skill.

Informal Conversation

Whether you meet engaged couples in a small-group setting or during the weekend retreat, there will be moments when you will interact informally with an individual or a couple. This happens, for example, when you first meet, during breaks, during a meal, and so on. What we know from research on Millennials is that what this generation wants is personal attention. These interactions are opportunities for the mentors to connect with the couples and give personal attention.

- Be friendly and sincere.
- Ask questions. Inquire about how the couple met, their plans for the wedding, or where they will live after the wedding. Ask about the schools they attended, the work they are doing, their hobbies, and so on.
- Listen attentively and with interest.
- Share information your own background, your school, your work, your family, where you got married, hobbies, and so on.
- Find something you have in common.

The purpose of all this is to show a genuine interest and care for the person or the couple. If you can connect with the couples whom you mentor, they will be more likely to listen to you with interest and will be more open to the message of the program.

Deliver Input on Various Topics and Share Your Experiences

Whether you are mentoring in small-group meetings or in weekend retreat sessions, you will be presenting information on specific topics. The *Mentor Guide* will provide you with talking points. In your delivery, consider the following:

- Deliver the information in your own words. In other words, do not read your notes.
- Whenever possible, follow the presentation of an important concept with an anecdote or an example from your life or from a story in the *Couple's Book*. This will help anchor the messages in the audience's mind.
- When possible, engage the participants with questions. These create interactions between you and the members of the group that foster interest and build the relationship.
- Try to keep a fifty-fifty balance between the time spent in presenting and the time spent in sharing your experiences.

Guide the Engaged Couples to Make the Best Use of Their Time during Their Personal Reflection and Private Sharing

In both formats the engaged couples will be given time for personal reflection and private sharing. This is their time, and it is important that you give them clear direction and sufficient time.

- Begin by giving the couples clear directions on what they are supposed to do. The *Mentor Guide* provides guidance on doing this.
- If your small group is meeting in your home, you may choose to leave the room during this time to allow for more privacy. If you are meeting with more than one engaged couple, think about where some of them might go to have at least some privacy.
- When the time runs out, let the couples know that they can continue their sharing later, on their own.

Facilitate Group Sharing

Both formats encourage devoting time for group sharing. The sharing is generally prompted by the mentor couple asking a question and waiting for someone to contribute by answering.

- This is not the time for you to continue your presentation. Your role is to encourage an exchange of ideas among the engaged couples.
- Throughout all of this, always listen and avoid statements that are judgmental.
- Present what Catholics believe or the facts reported by social sciences with a respectful attitude toward those who may disagree.

Special Circumstances

There may be times when you notice that a question causes a couple to feel uneasy. For example, you may find that a couple ends their private-sharing portion of the meeting with one or both visibly upset. Or you may find, from comments made during the group sharing or from questions that a couple asks, that a couple is upset or defensive.

Remember that your role is not to be a counselor or the judge of whether the couple is ready to marry. You are a mentor and a companion on their journey. You do what friends do. In situations such as these, let the couple know of what you notice, and then listen. For example, you might say, "We notice that you seem upset. Is something bothering one of you? Did we say anything, or did any of the questions you discussed bring up differences of opinion that are unsettling?" Depending on the answer you receive, you may suggest that they speak with the priest or deacon who is preparing them for the wedding.

If the problem persists over several sessions, you may approach the program director for guidance.

V. Time for Reflection and Practice

We recommend that the program director or the person leading the training of mentor couples designate at least one hour in the schedule to help mentor couples experience the program in the same way that the engaged couples will. During this time, using the *Mentor Guide*, the trainer walks through the materials of meeting 1. In other words, the trainer models the role of the mentor couple to those being trained.

VI. Closing

1. You Are Not Alone

Close the training by reminding the mentor couples that they are not alone in this ministry.

If they need help, the program director and the priest or deacon are ready to help.

The mentor couples are members of a ministry team and should feel free to reach out to one another for help.

Tell them that the parish community stands behind them.

> The parish will hold a commissioning ceremony during one of the Sunday Masses (give the date if one has been set).
>
> The parish will also offer prayers for the engaged couples and the mentor couples during the Universal Prayer at Sunday Masses.
>
> The parish will assign a prayer partner for each engaged couple.

2. The Role of the Holy Spirit

Encourage the mentor couples themselves to pray to the Holy Spirit. It is the Holy Spirit who prepares the engaged couples through the ministry of the parish community.

Ongoing Training for Mentors

While the training of mentor couples can start with an initial event as outlined above, it is important that such training be ongoing. It can be carried out through articles sent by the program director to the mentor couples or by holding a half-day or full-day retreat once a year. These retreats serve as a way to express the parish's gratitude for the team's service, and as an enrichment of the mentor couples' own marriages.

Close with the prayer to the Holy Spirit found in the *Mentor Guide*, page 54.

Support for Mentor Couples

Be sure to encourage everyone involved in marriage-preparation ministry in your parish to read the section "A Look at Engaged Couples Today" that begins on page 7 of the *Mentor Guide*. Today's engaged couples have needs that are unique to the millennial generation. In order to meet them where they are, we need to understand the situations that they bring to the parish when they ask for marriage in the Church. This information is also available at JoinedbyGrace.com.

Other important tools for the team to read are articles on ministering to couples in which one person is not Catholic and to couples who are already living together. These tools for team members also have companion articles that can be printed for engaged couples or that mentors can direct couples to at JoinedbyGrace.com.
Look for the following articles:

- "Ministering to Couples from Different Christian Communities or Different Religions"
- "A Welcome to Those Who Aren't Catholic"
- "Ministering to Couples Who Are Living Together"
- "Living Together before Marriage"

Premarital Inventories

Some pastoral ministers are finding premarital inventories useful for helping couples understand each other's values and habits and explore the areas of opportunity and difference. Many parishes have staff members trained to administer and guide the couple using these tools. Readiness for marriage cannot be scientifically measured, but an inventory helps those who are preparing couples for marriage ensure that the engaged couple discusses key issues that are important, not only for their readiness, but also for the validity of their marriage. These inventories are not tests that define readiness, but rather they are instruments that prompt discussion on issues that are important and sometimes sensitive. There are several excellent inventories on the market that are currently used by parishes. Below are four examples, with information about each culled from their websites.

FACET is a tool for assessing the relationship of a couple planning to be married. It helps the couple find topics they have not discussed, and, with the encouragement of a facilitator, it enables them to have positive, productive conversations. FACET is not a test but an opportunity to keep communications moving in a positive direction between two people who plan to get married. FACET is available in English and in Spanish.

Find more information at FacetSite.com, call 207-775-4757, or contact by e-mail at contact@facetsite.com.

The FOCCUS© Pre-Marriage Inventory is a comprehensive, user-friendly, research-based tool available for use by lay individuals, couples, clergy, or professionals who are helping couples prepare for marriage, and who complete FOCCUS training as required to become certified FOCCUS Facilitators. The FOCCUS Inventory is designed to help engaged couples appreciate their unique relationship, learn more about themselves, and discuss topics important to a healthy, happy, lifelong marriage. Each couple responds to statements in a variety of topic areas by indicating their agreement, disagreement, or uncertainty with the statements. Their responses generate an individualized Couple Report, which allows a trained facilitator to meet with the couple and facilitate couple discussion in areas such as communication, problem-solving, religion, family and friends, careers, cohabitation, parenting, sexuality, finances, and more. FOCCUS is offered in a variety of languages and editions, which are tailored to the needs of couples preparing for marriage in Catholic, Christian, Orthodox, and nonreligious settings.

Learn more about this tool at FoccusInc.com, call 877-883-5422 or 402-827-3735, or e-mail foccus@foccusinc.com.

Fully Engaged is a Catholic catechetical premarital inventory designed to help engaged couples solidify the foundation upon which they, together with Christ, will build their sacrament of Marriage. Grounded in Church teaching and loaded with catechetical content, this dynamic premarital inventory is a trustworthy guide that meets the real challenges today's couples face.

Fully Engaged helps couples to grow in their Catholic identity by smoothly integrating Church teaching into its materials. The Facilitator Guide, for use by clergy and lay ministers, contains adequate references to sacred scripture, as well as magisterial and ecclesial documents. Fully Engaged carries a Nihil Obstat and Imprimatur.

With the Couple's Workbook and monthly follow-up e-mail, Fully Engaged seeks to ensure that the couple continues to grow in the sacrament of Marriage during their time of preparation and in the future.

Learn more about this tool at GetFullyEngaged.com. Call 800-624-9019 or 320-252-4721 to order a preview kit, or e-mail fe@gw.stcdio.org

PREPARE/ENRICH is a relationship inventory and skill-building program used nationally and internationally. It is a nondenominational tool built on a solid research foundation. PREPARE/ENRICH is custom tailored to a couple's relationship and provides couple exercises to build their relationship skills.

The PREPARE/ENRICH Assessment is an online survey that a couple takes to help identify the unique strengths and potential growth areas of their premarital or married relationship. A trained facilitator, a counselor, or a certified pastor or priest must interpret the instrument. Spanish versions are available.

Learn more about this tool at Prepare-Enrich.com or call 800-331-1661.

4.

Marriage Preparation: A Ministry of the Whole Parish

> The complexity of today's society and the challenges faced by the family require a greater effort on the part of the whole Christian community in preparing those who are about to be married.
>
> —Pope Francis, *Amoris Laetitia*, 206

One of the unique features of Joined by Grace is that it looks at marriage preparation as an ongoing process within the parish community. In the life of the Church, marriage preparation is not intended to be an isolated event triggered by a couple's decision to marry, which culminates with the wedding. Marriage preparation is a continuous process that is taking place in the parish all the time.

Children and young people are being prepared for this vocation by what they learn in their homes, as well as in religious-education programs or Catholic schools. At home they learn about marriage by observing their parents. From their parents and other significant adults, they learn what it means to be a man or a woman, a father or a mother; they learn how husbands and wives interact with each other, and how the Christian faith guides and affects the relationship of husband and wife. Judith Siegel writes in her book *What Children Learn from Their Parents' Marriage,* "The marital relationship observed by the child acts like a blueprint upon which future intimate relationships will be built."[1] Similarly, St. John Paul II writes that marriage preparation begins in "early childhood" and is "a gradual and continuous process" (*Familiaris Consortio,* 66).

Marriage preparation is a ministry of the whole Christian community. St. John Paul II writes that the Christian family and the whole ecclesial community should feel involved in all the phases of this preparation (*Familiaris Consortio,* 66). To this purpose, Joined by Grace encourages pastoral ministers to invite the engaged couple and their families to a celebration and a blessing of their engagement. The revised *Order of Celebrating Matrimony* provides a beautiful "Order for Blessing an Engaged Couple." Learn more about this blessing at JoinedbyGrace.com.

We also encourage parishes formally to recognize the ministry to engaged couples with a commissioning ceremony for those who volunteer to be mentor couples. In addition, Joined by Grace approaches marriage preparation as a catechetical and educational opportunity for the whole community. Encourage the whole parish to pray for the engaged and to remember that marriage is a vocation. This chapter includes helpful resources and guidance on praying for both mentors and the engaged as a parish community.

The Pontifical Council for the Family expanded St. John Paul II's thoughts about the role of the community in marriage when it wrote, "It is desirable that the whole parish community take part in this celebration, around the families and friends of the engaged. Provisions for this should be made in various dioceses, taking local situations into account, but also decisively favoring truly ecclesial pastoral action."[2]

Joined by Grace encourages parishes to accompany the engaged couples as a community. Here are some of the ways in which the parish is actively involved in the preparation of the engaged:

- inviting married couples to be mentors
- commissioning the mentor couples during a Sunday Mass
- praying for the engaged couples and the mentor couples during the Universal Prayer/ Prayer of the Faithful at the Sunday liturgy
- assigning to each engaged couple one or more prayer partners

- announcing upcoming weddings in the parish bulletin and asking the whole parish to pray for the couples
- encouraging engaged couples to have their wedding during a Sunday Mass

In this section of the manual we provide tools and suggestions for involving the whole parish community in celebrating the blessing that is marriage. With these, the parish can support the couples who are preparing for marriage and those that accompany them on their journey. These tools are "Parish Website or Bulletin Announcements," "Blessing of Mentor Couples," "Blessing of an Engaged Couple," "Prayer Partners," "Online Resources and Short Articles," and "Additional Suggestions."

Parish Website or Bulletin Announcements

The parish website, bulletin, or app is the most basic tool for communication within a parish. In general, printed bulletins are accessible to anyone who attends Sunday Mass, and in many parishes they are also available online. This tool can therefore also become a vehicle for educating the parish about the importance of marriage and the family.

At JoinedbyGrace.com you will find a collection of fifty-two short inspirational quotations about marriage that can be inserted in the parish bulletin. We call this a "Marriage Matters" parish bulletin campaign. Most of the quotations are taken from the official documents of the Catholic Church: *Gaudium et Spes*, *Familiaris Consortio*, the USCCB's *Marriage: Love and Life in the Divine Plan*, and *Amoris Laetitia*. The purpose of each of these short quotations is catechetical. Through them the whole parish is educated on the vocation of marriage, the importance of the family, and the role of parents in forming their children. Feel free to use these parish announcements in any order you think appropriate. Here are a few sample parish announcements:

1. Marriage Matters *because God created it.*

"God Himself is that author of marriage," and he has given it a purpose (*Marriage: Love and Life in the Divine Plan*, 7).

2. **Marriage Matters** *to the future of society and of the Church.*

"The welfare of the family is decisive for the future of the world and that of the Church" (*Amoris Laititia*, 31).

3. **Marriage Matters** *because from the love of spouses comes the gift of life.*

"By their very nature, the institution of matrimony itself and conjugal love are ordained for the procreation and education of children, and find in them their ultimate crown" (*Gaudium et Spes*, 48).

4. **Marriage Matters** *because it is a bond between a man and a woman.*

"The Church has taught through the ages that marriage is an exclusive relationship between one man and one woman" (*Marriage: Love and Life in the Divine Plan*, 7).

5. **Marriage Matters** *because through it spouses become one.*

"Thus a man and a woman, who by the marriage covenant of conjugal love 'are no longer two, but one flesh' (Mt 19:6), render mutual help and service to each other through an intimate union of their persons and of their actions" (*Gaudium et Spes*, 48).

Blessing of Mentor Couples

Another way to involve the whole parish community in appreciating the importance and value of the marriage vocation and of marriage preparation is to have a blessing and sending ceremony for mentor couples. We urge that this occur during a Sunday Mass as it is an opportunity to involve the wider parish community in the marriage-preparation process as well as affirm and strengthen mentors in their ministry.

Sample

Prior to the opening hymn, the priest celebrant, a deacon, program director, or other parish minister, announces the special occasion using the following statement or something similar.

Priest or other minister:

The Church cares about the health of all marriages and places great importance on the preparation of couples for married life. In this parish we ask that, when couples become engaged, they begin their formal marriage-preparation process by contacting the parish office. They will be accompanied in their preparation by a member of the pastoral staff; by a mentor couple who will meet with them and share their experiences of marriage; and by us, the faith community, who will pray for them.

Today we will commission the married couples who will mentor the engaged. We give thanks to God for calling them to this ministry, and we pray that the Holy Spirit will grant them the graces they need in their ministry.

Mentor couples process in the entrance procession and are seated near the altar, but in the main body of the assembly.

Following the Liturgy of the Word, the presiding priest, a deacon, or the program director calls the mentor couples, preferably by name, to come forward.

Priest:

Dear couples [or (N and N)], you have been called to minister to engaged couples at (name of parish).

Are you willing to minister as mentor couples to those preparing for marriage?

Mentor Couples:

Yes, we are.

Priest:

May God pour out his blessing upon you

help you and guide you in your generous role,
and may he grant you all the graces you need
for this crucial ministry of the Church.
For your needs and the needs of all the Church,
we now turn to the Lord in his kindness.

The Universal Prayer follows in the usual manner. The following intercessions may be used in whole or in part. Feel free to write your own, following the usual pattern of these petitions.

Reader:

For the Church: May it grow stronger through the love of husband and wife and the families they create.

For this, we pray to the Lord: . . .

For the leaders of nations: May they protect marriage the way God created it, as an exclusive relationship between one man and one woman.

For this, we pray to the Lord: . . .

For the couples preparing for marriage in our parish this year: May God guide them in their discernment and help them prepare for the sacrament of Marriage.

For this, we pray to the Lord: . . .

For the families in our parish and throughout the world: May they grow stronger in their love and in their commitment to one another.

For this, we pray to the Lord: . . .

For those who suffer, especially the couples and families facing stressful situations and conflicts: May God comfort them, give them strength, and heal them through his infinite mercy.

For this, we pray to the Lord: . . .

[Other petitions may be added.]

Priest:

Lord God,

Creator of all that is good
and source of all love,
you sent your Son, Jesus Christ,
to live among us,
to proclaim the Good News,
and to teach us to love.
In your goodness
bless these couples
who have offered to serve your Church
as mentors to those who are preparing for the sacrament of Christian marriage.
Fill them with your Spirit
so that they may be
true sacraments of your love to the engaged.
We ask this through Christ our Lord.
Amen.

Blessing of an Engaged Couple

Blessings are a common spiritual practice in our Catholic tradition. Engagement is an important time in the life of a couple. It is a time of discernment and of intense immediate preparation to enter the sacrament of Marriage. Because of this, the families of the engaged couple and the couple themselves are encouraged to ask God for his guidance and blessings.

The *Book of Blessings*, prepared by the International Commission on English in the Liturgy, states, "The betrothal of a young Christian couple . . . is a special occasion for their families, who should celebrate it together with prayer and a special rite. In this way they ask God's blessing that the happiness promised by the children's engagement will be brought to fulfillment."[3] The *Book of Blessings* states that the parents of the engaged or a priest or deacon can lead this blessing. The ceremony can be held in various settings and occasions, but never during Mass. "Neither a formal betrothal nor the special blessing of an engaged couple is ever to be combined with the celebration of Mass."[4]

We recommend using or adapting the blessing found in the *Book of Blessings*, the "Order of Blessing an Engaged Couple" found in *The Order of Celebrating Matrimony*, or the ones found in *Catholic Household Blessings and Prayers* published by the USCCB Committee on Divine Worship. You can also use the short prayer found here, which is adapted from *Prayers for the Domestic Church* by Fr. Edward Hays.[5] This prayer can be led by a family member or by a deacon or priest.

Prayer for an Engaged Couple

Leader:

In the name of the Father, and of the Son, and of the Holy Spirit.

Lord our God,

We praise you and honor you, the source of all love.

We ask your blessing upon (N and N),

as they prepare for the sacred union of marriage.

We pray that they may best use this time of engagement

to grow in love and knowledge of one another.

May it be a time of great joy and rich blessings

and also a time of mature discernment.

(N and N), know of our prayers for you.

May you find the grace

to lovingly and deeply explore the challenges

as well as the joys that may lie ahead,

so that you can freely take up and embrace

a deep-rooted and lasting commitment of matrimony.

May these days of engagement be enriched with affection, grace, and peace.

May the fullness of God's blessing be upon you,

and grant you all the gifts you may need
during this special time in your life.
In the name of the Father, and of the Son, and of the Holy Spirit.
Amen.

Prayer Partners

As mentioned in chapter 2, the strongest support a parish community can offer couples preparing for marriage is prayer. Marriage preparation is a time of discernment and of decision making that affects the lives of many people, not just the couple. Marrying in the Church is an act of faith. The faith of a couple contributes to their success. Pope Benedict XVI said, "There is a clear link between the crisis in faith and the crisis in marriage."[6]

Invite individual parish members, couples, and families to become prayer partners with the engaged couples preparing for marriage. Assign to each of them an engaged couple who is participating in the program. The commitment of the prayer partners will be to pray each day for the engaged couple until the day of the wedding, and possibly into the future. Encourage them to write to the engaged couple, telling them that they are praying for them. The program director may act as a go-between in this communication, or with the permission of the engaged couple, give their address to the prayer partners. Invite the prayer partners to stay in contact with the engaged couple after the wedding, if they feel comfortable doing so. A card or e-mail from someone praying for them may be a ray of sunshine for the couple, especially if it arrives during a difficult moment in the early months after the wedding.

You may consider assigning a prayer partner to the mentor couples as well. They need the guidance of the Holy Spirit in carrying out their ministry.

In chapter 5 of this manual and at JoinedbyGrace.com you will find a sample note that you can use as you connect prayer partners to engaged couples. The note contains a prayer for daily use by the prayer partners as they support the engaged couples with whom they are connected.

Online Resources and Short Articles

Leading the parish toward a greater appreciation of the vocation of marriage can be done in many different ways. We mentioned previously the use of the parish bulletin and website, as well as prayers and blessings during Mass. The parish Facebook page, app, or newsletter are also great tools for this evangelizing work of the parish. We offer a collection of short articles on various aspects of married life, available to you and your parish team at JoinedbyGrace.com.

Additional Suggestions

The aim of Joined by Grace is to provide a sound preparation for engaged couples with the help of mentor couples and the clergy, and with the support of the whole parish. Here are some additional suggestions for involving the rest of the parish.

Publish the Names of Couples Preparing for Marriage

To involve the parish community in supporting those preparing for marriage, we suggest inserting in the parish bulletin the names of the couples who are preparing for marriage. Together with the names, include an invitation to the whole parish to pray for these couples and for those who are helping them prepare. This can be an ongoing box in the bulletin that gets updated as necessary, or it can be an announcement once a month with the names of those preparing for marriage at that time.

Special Intention during the Mass

You may want to include a special intention in the Universal Prayer of the Mass once a month.

- "For the members of our parish that are currently preparing to enter the sacrament of matrimony, and for those who are guiding them . . ."

- "For all married couples in the parish, that they grow in their vocation to serve God by loving each other . . ."

Encourage Couples to Celebrate Their Wedding during Sunday Mass

When local custom permits this, celebrating a wedding during Sunday Mass is the clearest way to express the communal dimension of the sacrament of Marriage. The wedding can truly become a communal celebration. After the Mass, the newlyweds and their families proceed to their private reception and parties.

Blessings for Married Couples

The Order of Celebrating Matrimony provides a beautiful blessing for the anniversary of marriage. *The Order* places this blessing within Sunday Mass. Utilizing this is a wonderful way to involve the whole parish in the work of marriage ministry.

5.

Tools

Sample Correspondence

In this chapter, you will find several sample letters that you can use to correspond with the engaged couples and members of the marriage-preparation team. Here you will find the following documents:

- Welcoming Letters to the Engaged Couples
- Invitation to the Informational Meeting for Mentor Couples
- Note to Prayer Partners
- Letter Introducing a Newly Married Couple to a New Pastor

Welcoming Letters to the Engaged Couples

Use one of these or a similar letter to invite the engaged couples to attend the marriage-preparation small-group meetings or weekend retreat. This letter may be sent by the program director, by the mentor couple, or by the lead couple for the weekend retreat.

Welcoming Letter for a Small-Group Format

Dear Engaged Couple,

Welcome to your preparation for the sacrament of marriage.

We are (N and N), members of (name of parish). We will be your mentor couple and are glad that you have chosen to be married in the Catholic Church. In the coming weeks, we will walk along with you on your journey to the altar, and we will pray for you after your wedding as you begin your life together as a married couple.

During our meetings, we will share with you some of our experiences of married life and how our faith has been a source of strength and guidance during our own marriage journey.

We ask you to participate as fully as possible in this program by attending each session, reading the materials assigned, and sharing honestly with each other your thoughts and feelings on the subjects presented during our meetings.

Your engagement is a time of discernment and preparation. Pope Francis said to a group of engaged couples that marriage is a relationship that is not just based on mere emotions, but a relationship that is "built in the same way that we build a house. And we build a house together, not alone! You should not wish to build it on shifting sands of emotions, but on the rock of true love, the love that comes from God."

We look forward to spending time with you while you build your relationship and prepare for marriage.

Important facts:

We will meet at: ______________________________

On the following dates: ______________________________

Start time: ______________ End time: ______________

Our e-mail address(es): ______________________________

Our phone number(s): ______________________________

Welcoming Letter for a Weekend Retreat

Dear Engaged Couple,

Welcome to your preparation for the sacrament of marriage.

We are (N and N), members of (name of parish). We will be directing the upcoming marriage-preparation weekend that you are scheduled to attend. We are glad that you have chosen to be married in the Catholic Church, and we look forward to meeting you and getting to know you during the retreat, which will take place on (dates) at (location).

The retreat will be led by a team of couples who will share with you their experiences of married life and how their faith has been a source of strength and guidance during their own marriage journeys.

We ask you to prepare for this special event by reading as many chapters as possible of the *Couple's Book* and sharing honestly with each other your thoughts and feelings about what you read.

Your engagement is a time of discernment and preparation. Pope Francis said to a group of engaged couples that marriage is a relationship that is not just based on mere emotions, but a relationship that is "built in the same way that we build a house. And we build a house together, not alone! You should not wish to build it on shifting sands of emotions, but on the rock of true love, the love that comes from God."

We look forward to spending time with you as you prepare for marriage.

Important facts:

We will meet at: ______________________________

On the following dates: ______________________________

The retreat starts at ____________ and will end at ____________.

Please be on time.

Our e-mail address(es): ______________________________

Our phone number(s): ______________________________

Invitation to the Informational Meeting for Mentor Couples

This sample letter is intended for potential mentor couples. It is written to invite candidates to an informational meeting during which they will learn about the program and their role in it, and hopefully they will make a commitment to be trained and to become a mentor couple.

Dear (N and N),

We begin by thanking you for agreeing to consider joining our pastor in the ministry to engaged couples as a mentor couple. Through this ministry, the Church prepares her children in their final steps to an important role in society and in the Church.

In this ministry you will be preparing couples to become the "domestic churches" of tomorrow. Because many couples initially come to the marriage-preparation program just to fulfill a requirement, your meeting with them is a great opportunity for the Church. They come to the Church and knock at her door asking for marriage. Sometimes they do not realize what they are asking. Your task in this ministry is to meet them where they are, walk with them, and guide them to the altar. Along the way, through your interactions you will show them what Christian marriage truly is. Your personal interest in them and the sharing of your faith and experiences of married life will open their eyes to what their relationship can be.

The pastor and I want to invite you to a brief informational meeting to explain to you the program we plan to use. We hope that with this knowledge you will commit to serve the parish in its ministry to engaged couples during the coming year.

Informational Meeting Date: ________________________________

Time: from ________________ to ________________________

Place: ____

Note to Prayer Partners

The strongest support a parish community can offer couples preparing for marriage is prayer. Marriage preparation is a time of discernment and of decision making that affects the lives of two people, as well as others. As mentioned above, marrying in the Church is an act of faith, and the faith of a couple contributes to their success. It's helpful to recall what Pope Benedict XVI said: "There is a clear link between the crisis in faith and the crisis in marriage."[1]

Invite and encourage parish members to be prayer partners for specific engaged couples who are attending the marriage-preparation program. Prayer partners can be any members of the parish; they need not be married. We encourage you to invite families to be prayer partners, since this could be a wonderful experience for children.

Here is a sample note you can send to the prayer partners. It is also available at JoinedbyGrace.com.

Dear (name of prayer partner),

Thank you for agreeing to be a prayer partner for a couple preparing for marriage at (name of parish). Your prayer is invaluable to our engaged couples during this crucial time of immediate preparation for marriage. This is a time of discernment and decision making and our engaged people can use the extra encouragement they will feel knowing you are praying for them. By marrying in the Church, couples embrace the vocation of Christian marriage, which is a call to be to be sacraments of God's love in the community and collaborators with God in bringing new life into the world.

Please pray the following prayer each day for (names of engaged couple). They will be married at (name of church) on (date).

Oh Lord, our God and Father,
We thank you for the gift of married love.
We ask your Spirit to open the hearts of (N and N),
and we ask your Son to teach them to love.
To grow in love and communion with you and with each other
is what they desire.
Grant them the will to welcome and accept each other,
the perseverance to keep their promise to always be present to each other,
and the generosity to give unselfishly day after day.

Grant (N and N) humility to ask forgiveness and courage to forgive,
compassion to console and strength to heal.
Grant them eagerness to serve without expecting to be served.
With your help, their unity will grow to resemble your communion,
and their hearts will be filled with joy.
This we ask through your Son, Jesus.
Amen.[2]

Please let me know if you have any questions or if I can be of help to you in this important ministry.

With deepest gratitude,

[Your name and contact information]

Letter Introducing a Newly Married Couple to a New Pastor

Often couples are prepared for marriage and marry in a parish, but then after the wedding they relocate to a different parish or to a different city. It is important that they remain connected to the Church during such transitions.

Use the following note as a guide in creating a simple communication through which the pastor introduces a relocating couple to the new pastor and pastoral staff. The hope is that the new parish will reach out to this couple and welcome them, inviting them to become involved in the life of the community.

Dear Pastor,

I am writing to introduce to you a young married couple who has just relocated from our parish to yours. They were married here at (name of parish) on (date) and participated in our marriage-preparation program, Joined by Grace. Our prayers go with them, and we hope that they will find in your community the support they need to live out their married vocation.

If it is possible to have someone from your staff or a couple from your parish contact them and welcome them, it will be appreciated.

Their information is as follows:

Name: ______________________________

Street Address: ______________________________

E-mail Address(es): ______________________________

Phone number(s): ______________________________

Respectfully,

[Your name and contact information]

Program Evaluation Forms

Small-Group Format

Date of First Meeting: ___________ Date of Last Meeting: _____________

Name of parish where you will be married: ______________________________________

Name of mentor couple: ____

What did you find *most* helpful in this program?

What did you find *least* helpful in this program?

What did you learn that was new to you?

What did you learn in this program that you want to remember for years to come?

Additional Comments:

Names: ____

We would like to stay in contact with you. Would you give us your information?

Street address after the wedding: ____

Phone number(s): ____

E-mail address(es): ____

Weekend Retreat Format

Dates of retreat: ________________

Name of parish where you will be married: ____

What did you find *most* helpful in this program?

What did you find *least* helpful in this program?

What did you learn that was new to you?

What did you learn in this program that you want to remember for years to come?

Additional Comments:

Names: ____

We would like to stay in contact with you. Would you give us your information?

Street address after the wedding: ____

Phone number(s): ____

E-mail address(es): ____

6.

After the Wedding

Resources for Newly Married Couples

The Census Bureau reports that in 2009 first marriages that ended in divorce lasted a median of eight years.[1] The early years are the most difficult for most couples. Ted Huston, PhD, a professor of human ecology and psychology at the University of Texas at Austin, through a long-term study of married couples, found that the first two years of marriage are the most important in helping couples define patterns of behaviors for their relationship. These patterns can either help the couple for the rest of their lives or can lead to divorce. In looking at predictors of success or divorce, he finds that what leads to divorce is not the presence of conflicts, but rather it is "disillusionment," the loss of "positive feelings" for one's spouse.[2] The aim of parish ministry to young married couples should be to help them nurture the respect and appreciation for each other that they discovered during their dating years.

The Catholic Church recognizes that newly married couples are most vulnerable in the early years of adjustment to married life. St. John Paul II wrote in *Familiaris Consortio*, "The pastoral care of regularly established families signifies, in practice, the commitment of all the members of the local ecclesial community. . . . This holds true especially for young families, which . . . are more vulnerable, especially in the first years of marriage" (69). Similar thoughts were expressed in the interventions of bishops and experts during the two synods on the family in 2014 and 2015 as well as by Pope Francis in *Amoris Laetitia*: "The Synod Fathers observed that 'the initial years of marriage are a vital and sensitive period during which couples become more aware of the challenges and meaning of married life. Consequently, pastoral accompaniment needs to go beyond the actual celebration of the sacrament'" (223).

Pope Francis continues by emphasizing that the parish is the place where experienced couples can help younger couples. He writes that young couples should be encouraged to develop a routine of daily rituals, such as "a morning kiss, and evening blessing, waiting at the door to welcome each other home, taking trips together and sharing household chores." He encourages families to celebrate anniversaries and special events. "We need these moments of cherishing God's gifts and renewing our zest for life" (226).

He advises those who work with young couples "Emphasis should also be given to the importance of family spirituality, prayer, and participation in the Sunday Eucharist" (223). Social scientists agree with the Pope regarding the importance of regular church attendance to the happiness of a couple. The Institute for Family Studies published a report by Dr. Bradford Wilcox and Nicholas Wolfinger that found that 78 percent of couples who regularly attended religious services together are very or extremely happy in their marriage. [3] The following resources may assist your parish in supporting the newlywed couples in your community.

Newsletters

Together for Life Online

This monthly newsletter, published by Ave Maria Press, can be obtained free of charge by subscribing at TogetherforLifeOnline.com.

For Your Marriage

ForYourMarriage.org is a website dedicated to marriage and family life. It includes articles, book reviews, blogs, and resources that married couples can use to strengthen their relationships. Sponsored by the United States Conference of Catholic Bishops (USCCB), it provides help for both Catholics and anyone interested in preparing, sustaining, or repairing their marriage. This website offers a free monthly newsletter containing information and inspiration for couples. Visit ForYourMarriage.org to subscribe.

Por Tu Matrimonio

This is a website similar to ForYourMarriage.org but in Spanish. It also delivers a monthly newsletter in Spanish that offers information and inspiration for couples. Visit PorTuMatrimonio.org to subscribe.

FOUNDATIONS

The goal of this bimonthly newsletter is "to offer resources for couples starting on the journey of married life. No matter how old you are or what your previous experience is, if you are beginning a marriage you have some unique challenges and opportunities ahead of you." This newsletter is available for a small fee at FacetSite.com/foundations/index.html.

Books

An extensive list of books and articles for married couples is available at the USCCB website ForYourMarriage.org/books-articles/.

Beirne, Steve, and Kathy Beirne. *Catholic and Newly Married: 5 Challenges and 5 Opportunities*. Chicago: ACTA Publications, 2012.
This book is aimed toward couples who are about to be or have recently married. It is meant to help in the transition from single life to the happy, healthy married state.

Bosio, John. *Blessed Is Marriage: A Guide to the Beatitudes for Catholic Couples*. New London, CT: Twenty-Third Publications, 2012.
John Bosio draws from his experience as a family therapist and committed believer to provide a path for a loving marriage inspired by the Beatitudes. He proclaims the importance of the promises made and kept in marriage and offers couples both theological and biblical grounding as well as inspiration as they seek to strengthen their marriage commitment.

———. *Happy Together: The Catholic Blueprint for a Loving Marrige*. London, CT: Twenty-Third Publications, 2008.

Bosio challenges couples to overcome selfishness by learning to love each other as Christ loves. He identifies and focuses on six key aspects of a loving marriage, and he uses stories and examples to illustrate each. This is an open, realistic, and encouraging book about marriage. It is highly recommended for married couples, engaged couples, and marriage-enrichment groups.

Hahn, Kimberly. *Life-Giving Love: Embracing God's Beautiful Design for Marriage*. Cincinnati, OH: Servant Books, 2001.

God has a beautiful design for your marriage. Have you discovered it? Blueprints for building a family seem to abound today. But the countless plans proposed don't all agree, and married couples are often left confused. Where can we turn for a true vision of what it takes to build happy, healthy, holy families?

Popcak, Gregory K. *Holy Sex! A Catholic Guide to Toe-Curling, Mind-Blowing, Infallible Loving*. New York: The Crossroad Publishing Company, 2008.

Common wisdom portrays sex and the Church to be at odds, yet studies show that Catholics have better sex and more often. This witty, frank, and refreshingly orthodox book draws from the beautiful truths of Catholic teaching to show people of all faiths about rich and satisfying sexuality. Hailed by Christians across the spectrum from Christopher West and Janet E. Smith to John L. Allen Jr., *Holy Sex!* includes dozens of questionnaires, quizzes, and valuable lessons from real-life stories.

Popcak, Greg, and Lisa Popcak. *Just Married: The Catholic Guide to Surviving and Thriving in the First Five Years of Marriage*. Notre Dame, IN: Ave Maria Press, 2013.

In this book, Greg and Lisa Popcak combine decades of counseling, the latest findings in marriage research, more than twenty years of marriage, and the wisdom of Catholic teaching to offer couples the most up-to-date look at what it takes to create and sustain an incredible Catholic marriage that will last a lifetime.

Sheen, Fulton J. *Three to Get Married*. New Rochelle, NY: Scepter Publishers, 1996.

One of the greatest and best-loved spokesmen for the Catholic faith here sets out the Church's beautiful understanding of marriage in his trademark clear and entertaining style. Frankly and charitably, Sheen presents the causes of and solutions to common marital crises, and tells touching real-life stories of people whose lives were transformed through marriage. He emphasizes that our Blessed Lord is at the center of every successful and loving marriage. This is a perfect gift for engaged couples, or for married people as a fruitful occasion for self-examination.

Hays, Edward. *Prayers for the Domestic Church: Handbook for Worship in the Home*. Notre Dame, IN: Ave Maria Press, 2007.

First published in 1979, this groundbreaking book established Edward Hays as a pioneering spiritual writer and teacher, and it has since sold more than 150,000 copies. This new edition with a new preface by the author celebrates the "domestic church"—a family worshiping together at home—with a collection of prayers and blessings that remain as fresh and creative today as they were more than twenty-five years ago. With blessings for birthdays, family members, the home, pets, and more, this book makes it easy and fun to gather in prayer as a family. This book is an ideal gift for weddings, baptisms, the birth of a child, special family milestones, and sacred moments.

United States Conference of Catholic Bishops. *Catholic Household Blessings and Prayers*. New York: Image, 2012.

Families will use *Catholic Household Blessings and Prayers* to learn essential prayers that Catholics need to know; to celebrate the feasts and seasons of the Church year in ritual and prayer; to bless the Advent wreath, Christmas crèche, and Easter foods; to lead grace before and after meals; to pray for family members; and to bless the home before a move and in times of trouble.

Parish Programs

In addition to books, the USCCB website ForYourMarriage.org provides an extensive list of programs for marriage enrichment as well as for support of marriages experiencing difficulties. Visit ForYourMarriage.org/marriage-programs/. Here are some of the programs listed.

Six Dates for Catholic Couples by John and Teri Bosio

http://www.happy-together.net/six-dates-for-catholic-couples/

Building and strengthening marriages begins with husbands and wives making time to be with each other and to have fun together. The companion book and the videos inspire spouses to become aware of the gift that they are to each other as husband and wife while encouraging them to make going on dates a habit in their relationship. The program is designed for couples to use at home on their own, or for parishes to sponsor date-night programs as community events. This program is highly recommended because it is a perfect follow-up to Joined by Grace. The view of marriage portrayed in Joined by Grace was first developed in the book *Happy Together: The Catholic Blueprint for a Loving Marriage* and the *Six Dates for Catholic Couples* program.

The Beatitudes: A Couple's Path to Greater Joy by John and Teri Bosio.
http://www.happy-together.net/the-beatitudes-a-couples-s-path-to-greater-joy/

This marriage-enrichment program explores the Beatitudes as the path to holiness in Christian marriage. Holiness is the source of joy in marriage. The companion book and the videos guide married couples to live the Beatitudes in their daily lives. The program is designed to be used as a date-night program with six topics, or as a group discussion among couples.

Together with Jesus: Couple Prayer Series by Bob and Kathy Ovies
http://www.coupleprayer.com/#!series/c1xu8

The *Couple Prayer* series was created to help married or engaged couples come together in ways they'll find to be safe, gradual, and genuinely successful in order to discover the life-changing intimacy of being able to pray together closely, openly, and honestly as a basic part of their marriage relationship. Videos provide a world of information and suggestions about the "whats," "whys," and "how-tos" of proven shared-prayer experiences, while the personal stories of couples whose lives have been transformed by couple prayer provide strong encouragements throughout the series.

Ministry to the Newly Married by Agape Catholic Ministries
http://www.agapecatholicministries.com/ministry-to-the-newly-married

This five-year parish-based mentoring program for newlywed couples offered by Agape Catholic Ministries pairs new married couples with couples married at least five years, with the goal of fostering the new couple's relationship skills and broadening their understanding of each other as they live out the sacrament of Marriage.

National Marriage Encounter
http://marriage-encounter.org

National Marriage Encounter promotes and encourages marriage and family life by offering Marriage Encounter weekends and a support community. It is open to couples of all faiths and to those of no religious affiliation.

Worldwide Marriage Encounter
http://www.wwme.org
Worldwide Marriage Encounter is a weekend experience that teaches a technique of loving communication to promote intimate and responsible relationships, and it offers community support for the sacramental lifestyle modeled by the presenters. The experience is offered in several languages.

Teams of Our Lady
http://www.teamsofourlady.org/home0.aspx
This movement of married spirituality brings together Christian couples united by the sacrament of marriage who wish, together, to deepen the graces of their lives within the sacrament of marriage.

Notes

1. Exploring the Vision of Joined by Grace

1. Covenant Eyes, "Pornography Statistics: 250+ Facts, Quotes, and Statistics about Pornography Use," 2015 ed. (Owosso, MI: Covenant Eyes, 2015), 18.

2. Mark M. Gray, "Catholic Schools Linked to Church Vitality," *The Cara Report* 20, no. 3 (Washington, DC: Center for Applied Research in the Apostolate, Georgetown University, Winter 2015).

3. Ibid.

4. Mark M. Gray, Paul M. Perl, and Tricia C. Bruce, *Marriage in the Catholic Church: A Survey of U.S. Catholics* (Washington, DC: Center for Applied Research in the Apostolate, Georgetown University, October 2007).

5. William V. D'Antonio, Michele Dillon, and Mary L. Gautier, *American Catholics in Transition* (New York: Rowman & Littlefield, 2013), 144.

6. Jeff Fromm and Christine Garton, *Marketing to Millennials* (New York: American Management Association, 2013), 9.

7. *15 Economic Facts about Millennials* (Washington, DC: The Council of Economic Advisers, October 2014).

2. Implementing the Program in Your Parish

1. "Canon 1063," *Code of Canon Law: Latin-English Translation* (Washington, DC: Canon Law Society of America, 1983), 389.

2. Ibid.

3. "Canon 1066," *Code of Canon Law*, 391.

4. Jay Biber, "The Role of Clergy in Marriage Preparation," USCCB, http://www.usccb.org/issues-and-action/marriage-and-family/marriage/marriage-preparation/upload/Biber.pdf.

5. Benedict XVI, "Address of His Holiness Pope Benedict XVI on the Occasion of the Inauguration of the Judicial Year of the Tribunal of the Roman Rota," January 22, 2011, https://w2.vatican.va/content/benedict-xvi/en/speeches/2011/january/documents/hf_ben-xvi_spe_20110122_rota-romana.html.

6. Francis, "Address of Pope Francis to Engaged Couples Preparing for Marriage," February 14, 2014, https://w2.vatican.va/content/francesco/en/speeches/2014/february/documents/papa-francesco_20140214_incontro-fidanzati.html.

3. Recruiting and Training Mentor Couples

1. Pontifical Council for the Family, "Preparation for the Sacrament of Marriage," May 13, 1996, no. 43, http://www.vatican.va/roman_curia/pontifical_councils/family/documents/rc_pc_family_doc_13051996_preparation-for-marriage_en.html.

4. Marriage Preparation: A Ministry of the Whole Parish

1. Judith P. Siegel, *What Children Learn from Their Parents' Marriage: It May Be Your Marriage, but It's Your Child's Blueprint for Intimacy* (New York: Harper Perennial, 2001), xvi.

2. Pontifical Council for the Family, "Preparation for the Sacrament of Marriage," May 13, 1996, no. 54, http://www.vatican.va/roman_curia/pontifical_councils/family/documents/rc_pc_family_doc_13051996_preparation-for-marriage_en.html.

3. International Commission on English in the Liturgy, "Blessings of an Engaged Couple," *Book of Blessings* (Collegeville, MN: Liturgical Press, 1989), par. 195.

4. Ibid., par. 198.

5. Edward Hays, *Prayers for the Domestic Church: Handbook for Worship in the Home* (Notre Dame, IN: Ave Maria Press, 2007), 123.

6. Benedict XVI, "Homily of His Holiness Pope Benedict XVI," October 7, 2012, http://w2.vatican.va/content/benedict-xvi/en/homilies/2012/documents/hf_ben-xvi_hom_20121007_apertura-sinodo.html.

5. Tools

1. Benedict XVI, "Homily of His Holiness Pope Benedict XVI, October 7, 2012, http://w2.vatican.va/content/benedict-xvi/en/homilies/2012/documents/hf_ben-xvi_hom_20121007_apertura-sinodo.html.

2. This prayer is adapted from John Bosio, *Happy Together: The Catholic Blueprint for a Loving Marriage* (London, CT: Twenty-Third Publications, 2008), 5.

6. After the Wedding

1. United States Census Bureau, *Number, Timing, Duration of Marriages and Divorces: 2009*, 15.

2. Aviva Patz, "Will Your Marriage Last?" *Psychology Today*, January 1, 2000, https://www.psychologytoday.com/articles/200001/will-your-marriage-last.

3. W. Bradford Wilcox and Nicholas H. Wolfinger, Better Together: Religious Attendance, Gender, and Relationship Quality, (Family Studies, February 11, 2016), sourced on July 7, 2016 at: Family-Studies.org/better-together-religious-attendance/.

John Bosio is active in marriage and family ministry, serving parishes and dioceses across the country. With his wife, Teri, he leads couples' retreats and family ministry workshops for deacons and priests. The couple has produced two parish-based marriage enrichment programs: *Six Dates for Catholic Couples* and *The Beatitudes: A Couple's Path to Greater Joy*. They are authors of several books, including *Happy Together* and *Blessed is Marriage*.

He earned his bachelor's degree in sacred theology from Catholic University and master's degrees in theology from St. Paul's College and education from the University of Missouri. He is a certified marriage and family therapist.

Bosio previously served as a private practice marriage and family therapist as well as a parish religious education director and diocesan family life coordinator. He is a member of the National Association for Marriage and Family Life Ministers. He and Teri have two daughters and a grandchild.

Teri Bosio is active in marriage and family ministry, serving parishes and dioceses across the country. With her husband, John, she leads couples' retreats and family ministry workshops for deacons and priests. The couple has produced two parish-based marriage enrichment programs: *Six Dates for Catholic Couples* and *The Beatitudes: A Couple's Path to Greater Joy*. They are authors of several books, including *Happy Together* and *Blessed is Marriage*.

Bosio previously worked as family life coordinator for the Archdiocese of Kansas City, a parish director of adult formation and RCIA, and as a parish religious education director. She earned her associate's degree from Johnson County Community College and her bachelor's degree from Trevecca Nazarene University. She is a member of the National Association of Marriage and Family Life Ministers. She and John have two daughters and a grandchild.

Joined by Grace

Discover additional resources at **JoinedbyGrace.com**

At JoinedbyGrace.com you will find articles, exercises, tools, and resources to share with the engaged couples.

For help planning and preparing for Catholic wedding ceremonies, visit TogetherforLifeOnline.com.